GREATEST EVER
Potato

This is a Papplewick Press Book
First published in 2002

Papplewick Press
Unit 5 Bestwood Business Park
Bestwood Village
Nottingham NG6 8AN, UK

ISBN: 0-75259-335-8

Printed in Dubai

NOTE

This book uses metric and imperial measurements. Follow the same units
of measurement throughout; do not mix metric and imperial.
All spoon measurements are level: teaspoons are assumed to be 5 ml,
and tablespoons are assumed to be 15 ml. Unless otherwise stated,
milk is assumed to be full fat, eggs and individual vegetables such as potatoes
are medium, and pepper is freshly ground black pepper.

Recipes using raw or very lightly cooked eggs should be
avoided by infants, the elderly, pregnant women, convalescents, and anyone
suffering from an illness.

Contents

Introduction

The potato is one of the world's most popular
vegetables, cultivated in almost every country. There
are many different varieties, native to these countries,
each having a different quality or property. As a result
of this, the potato suits most culinary styles and is

perhaps the most versatile staple food available. It is recognised as one of the
most important crops cultivated for human consumption, with Russia, Poland
and Germany being the highest consumers, closely followed by Holland,
Cyprus and Ireland.

We eat about 109 kg/242 lb per head per annum, which is good news
when you consider the nutritional properties of this best-loved tuber. A serving
of 225 g/8 oz of potatoes contains around 180 calories and provides us
with protein, energy-rich starch and fibre, as well as being a good source of
vitamin C. Most of the vitamins are found just beneath the skin, which is why
it is often suggested that potatoes are cooked in their skins and then peeled. If
not cooked with fat, the potato has a great role to play in the slimming diet, a
fact which has been disputed in the past.

Buying and Storing

When choosing potatoes, make sure they are firm and well-shaped with a smooth, tight skin. New potatoes should be eaten as fresh as possible, but old potatoes can be stored in a cool, dark, dry place – exposure to light makes them turn green, resulting in an unpleasant flavour and a higher level of glycoalkaloids, which are naturally occuring toxins.

Preparation and Cooking

To preserve the nutritional value of potatoes, they should be baked in their skins, or scrubbed rather than peeled. If peeled potatoes are required, they should be cooked in their skins and peeled afterwards.

Boiling

Suitable for waxy varieties, e.g. Wilja or Charlotte. For new and old potatoes, place them in a pan, pour in enough boiling water to cover, put on a lid and boil gently until tender.

Steaming

To steam new and old potatoes, place them in a steamer over a pan of boiling water and cook them gently until they are tender.

Mashing or Creaming

Suitable for floury varieties such as King Edward or Maris Piper. Boil the potatoes, then drain well. Add a knob of butter, season, then mash with a potato masher. Beat in sufficient hot milk with a fork or wooden spoon to give a creamy consistency. For a change, add a little crème fraîche or fresh pesto sauce.

Roasting

Suitable for both floury and waxy varieties. Par-boil the potatoes, return to the pan and heat for 3-4 minutes, shaking the pan to roughen the potato. Place in hot oil in a roasting tin and cook on the top shelf at 220°C/ 425°F/Gas Mark 7 for 45 minutes–1 hour until golden and crispy.

Frying

For cooking perfect chips, the temperature of the oil is all-important and a deep-fat fryer is a good investment. Par-boiled, sliced or diced potatoes can be fried or sautéed in a little oil in a heavy-based pan.

Baking

Most varieties will bake, but avoid those with thin skins . Scrub and prick the skins, and bake at 220°C/ 425°F/ Gas Mark 7 for 1–1½ hours.

Potato Varieties

There are many varieties of potato, but only about 100 of these are regularly grown.

Of these, about 30 are found with ease on our greengrocers' and supermarket shelves. The following is a

brief description of the types available, as a guide for the recipes in this book.

First Earlies

These are the first new potatoes, available in the spring and early summer. Varieties include Duke of York, a kidney shaped tuber with yellow flesh, and Rocket which has a white skin and flesh with a firm and waxy texture.

Cyprus New Potato

Available in late winter and spring, and best simply scrubbed and boiled.

Jersey Royal

Perhaps our most popular new potato, with a distinctive, earthy flavour, appearing from mid May to July.

Second Earlies

Traditionally, second earlies bridge the gap between the first earlies and the `maincrop' varieties which appear in autumn. Normally larger in size than the first earlies, some of the varieties (such as Estima) continue to be available into the maincrop season. Estima has a smooth, light yellow skin with a firm, moist flesh. It is suitable for roasting and baking. Maris Peer tubers have a white skin and flesh and excellent flavour. Wilja is a very popular variety. It has elongated or pear-shaped tubers with yellow firm flesh and skin.

Maincrop

Often referred to as 'old' potatoes. The tubers are mature and are normally larger than the other crops due to the longer growing time. They keep well throughout the winter in cool dark conditions. Varieties include King Edward – small oval tubers with pink and white skins, creamy flavoured flesh and floury texture and one of the most popular of all varieties. Maris Piper (also very popular and widely available) is a medium-firm potato with a creamy white floury flesh. Desirée is a red skinned potato with light yellow firm flesh and an all-round variety. Kerr's Pink is another red skinned potato, with large oval tubers and a light yellow, floury flesh.

Specialities
Pink Fir Apple has long, knobbly tubers with a yellow flesh and pink skin. The firm, waxy texture means it keeps well. The strong, robust flavour of this potato makes it ideal in salads. Anya has all the characteristics of Pink Fir Apple but it can also be used in casseroles,stews or served plain boiled.

White Sweet Potato
Smaller than the yam, this is yellow-fleshed with a dry texture. Best fried, boiled or casseroled, it is ideal with spices.

Yam
A red sweet potato which is orange-fleshed. Best mashed in cakes and soufflés or roasted.

Soups

Potatoes form the basis of many delicious and easy-to-prepare home-made soups because they are the perfect thickening agent, while adding a subtle flavour. With the addition of just a few ingredients, you can have a selection of soups at your fingertips. Add herbs, onion, garlic, meat, fish or vegetables, top with herbs or croûtons, and serve with crusty bread for anything from a light starter to a filling meal.

potato & mushroom soup

serves four

2 tbsp vegetable oil

600 g/1 lb 5 oz floury
   potatoes, sliced

1 onion, sliced

2 garlic cloves, crushed

1 litre/1¾ pints beef stock

25 g/1 oz dried mushrooms, soaked
   in hot water for 20 minutes

2 celery sticks, sliced

2 tbsp brandy

salt and pepper

TOPPING

3 tbsp butter

2 thick slices white bread,
   crusts removed

55 g/2 oz Parmesan cheese,
   freshly grated

TO GARNISH

dried mushrooms, soaked in
   hot water for 20 minutes
   and drained

fresh parsley sprigs

1 Heat the vegetable oil in a large frying pan and add the potatoes, onion and garlic. Sauté gently for 5 minutes, stirring constantly.

2 Add the beef stock, dried mushrooms and their strained soaking water and the celery. Bring to the boil, then reduce the heat to a simmer, cover the saucepan and cook the soup for 20 minutes, until the potatoes are tender.

3 Meanwhile, melt the butter for the topping in the frying pan. Sprinkle the bread slices with the grated cheese and fry the slices in the butter for 1 minute on each side, until crisp. Using a sharp knife, cut each slice into triangles.

4 Stir the brandy into the soup, and season to taste. Pour into warmed bowls and top with the triangles. Serve garnished with mushrooms and parsley.

COOK'S TIP

Probably the most popular dried mushroom is the cep, but any variety will add a lovely flavour to this soup. If you do not wish to use dried mushrooms, add 125 g/4½ oz sliced fresh mushrooms of your choice to the soup.

potato & chickpea soup

serves four

1 tbsp olive oil

1 large onion, chopped finely

2–3 garlic cloves, chopped finely
  or crushed

1 carrot, quartered and thinly sliced

350 g/12 oz potatoes, diced

¼ tsp ground turmeric

¼ tsp garam masala

¼ tsp mild curry powder

400 g/14 oz canned chopped
  tomatoes

850 ml/1½ pints water

¼ tsp chilli purée, or to taste

400 g/14 oz canned chickpeas,
  drained and rinsed

85 g/3 oz fresh or frozen peas

salt and pepper

chopped fresh coriander, to garnish

3 Add the tomatoes, measured water and chilli purée with a large pinch of salt. Reduce the heat, cover and simmer for 30 minutes, stirring occasionally.

4 Add the chickpeas and peas to the pan, then continue cooking for about 15 minutes, or until all the vegetables are tender.

5 Taste the soup and adjust the seasoning, if necessary, adding a little more chilli purée if you like. Ladle into warm individual soup bowls, sprinkle with chopped coriander and serve immediately.

1 Heat the olive oil in a large saucepan over a medium heat. Add the onion and garlic and cook, stirring occasionally, for 3–4 minutes, until the onion is beginning to soften.

2 Add the carrot, potatoes, turmeric, garam masala and curry powder and continue cooking for 1–2 minutes.

indian potato & pea soup

serves four

2 tbsp vegetable oil

225 g/8 oz floury potatoes, diced

1 large onion, chopped

2 garlic cloves, crushed

1 tsp garam masala

1 tsp ground coriander

1 tsp ground cumin

850 ml/1½ pints vegetable stock

1 fresh red chilli, deseeded
    and chopped

100 g/3½ oz frozen peas

4 tbsp natural yogurt

salt and pepper

chopped fresh coriander,
    to garnish

warm bread, to serve

2 Add the garam masala, ground coriander and cumin and cook, stirring constantly, for 1 minute.

4 Add the peas and cook for a further 5 minutes. Stir in the yogurt and season to taste with salt and pepper.

1 Heat the vegetable oil in a large saucepan. Add the potatoes, onion and garlic and sauté over a low heat, stirring constantly, for about 5 minutes.

3 Stir in the vegetable stock and red chilli and bring the mixture to the boil. Reduce the heat, cover the pan and simmer for 20 minutes, until the potatoes begin to break down.

5 Pour into warmed soup bowls, garnish with chopped fresh coriander and serve immediately with warm bread.

potato & vegetable soup with pistou

serves six

2 young carrots

450 g/1 lb potatoes

200 g/7 oz fresh peas in their pods

200 g/7 oz thin green beans

150 g/5½ oz young courgettes

2 tbsp olive oil

1 garlic clove, crushed

1 large onion, chopped finely

2.5 litres/4½ pints vegetable stock
   or water

1 bouquet garni of 2 fresh parsley
   sprigs and 1 bay leaf tied in a
   7.5-cm/3-inch piece of celery

85 g/3 oz dried small soup pasta

1 large tomato, skinned, deseeded
   and chopped or diced

Parmesan cheese shavings,
   to serve

PISTOU SAUCE

75 g/2¾ oz fresh basil leaves

1 garlic clove

5 tbsp fruity extra virgin olive oil

salt and pepper

1 To make the pistou sauce, put the basil leaves, garlic and olive oil in a food processor and process until well blended. Season with salt and pepper to taste. Transfer to a bowl, cover with clingfilm and chill until required.

2 Peel the carrots and cut them in half lengthways, then slice. Peel the potatoes and cut into quarters lengthways, then slice. Place in a bowl and cover with cold water until ready to use, to prevent discoloration.

3 Shell the peas. Top and tail the beans and cut them into 2.5-cm/ 1-inch pieces. Cut the courgettes in half lengthways, then slice.

4 Heat the oil in a large saucepan or flameproof casserole. Add the garlic and fry for 2 minutes, stirring. Add the onion and continue frying for

2 minutes, until soft. Add the carrots and potatoes and stir for about 30 seconds.

5 Pour in the stock or water and bring to the boil. Lower the heat, partially cover and simmer for 8 minutes, until the vegetables are starting to become tender.

6 Stir in the peas, beans, courgettes, bouquet garni, pasta and tomato. Season and cook for 8–10 minutes, or until tender. Discard the bouquet garni, stir in the pistou sauce and serve with the Parmesan.

leek, potato & bacon soup

serves four

2 tbsp butter

175 g/6 oz potatoes, diced

4 leeks, shredded

2 garlic cloves, crushed

100 g/3½ oz smoked bacon, diced

850 ml/1½ pints vegetable stock

225 ml/8 fl oz double cream

2 tbsp chopped fresh parsley

salt and pepper

TO GARNISH

vegetable oil

1 leek, shredded

1 Melt the butter in a large saucepan and add the potatoes, leeks, garlic and bacon. Sauté gently for 5 minutes, stirring constantly.

2 Add the vegetable stock and bring to the boil. Reduce the heat, cover the saucepan and simmer for 20 minutes until the potatoes are cooked. Stir in the double cream and mix well.

3 Meanwhile, make the garnish. Half-fill a pan with oil and heat to 180°C–190°C/350°F–375°F or until a cube of bread browns in 30 seconds. Add the shredded leek and deep-fry for 1 minute, until browned and crisp, taking care because it contains water. Drain the shredded leek thoroughly on kitchen paper and reserve.

4 Reserve a few pieces of potato, leek and bacon and set aside. Put the rest of the soup in a food processor or blender, in batches, and process each batch for 30 seconds. Return the puréed soup to a clean saucepan and heat through.

5 Stir in the reserved vegetables, bacon and parsley and season to taste. Pour into warmed bowls and garnish with the fried leeks.

VARIATION

For a lighter soup, omit the cream and stir yogurt or crème fraîche into the soup at the end of the cooking time.

chicken & vegetable soup

serves four

1 litre/1¾ pints chicken stock

175 g/6 oz skinless, boneless
   chicken breast

fresh parsley and tarragon sprigs

2 garlic cloves, crushed

125 g/4½ oz baby carrots, halved
   or quartered

225 g/8 oz small new
   potatoes, quartered

4 tbsp plain flour

125 ml/4 fl oz milk

4–5 spring onions, diagonally sliced

85 g/3 oz asparagus tips, halved
   and cut into 4-cm/1½-inch pieces

125 ml/4 fl oz whipping or
   double cream

1 tbsp finely chopped fresh parsley

1 tbsp finely chopped fresh tarragon

salt and pepper

1 Put the stock in a saucepan with the chicken, parsley and tarragon sprigs and garlic. Bring just to the boil, reduce the heat, cover and simmer for 20 minutes, or until the chicken is cooked through and firm to the touch.

2 Remove the chicken and strain the stock. When the chicken is cool enough to handle, cut into bite-sized pieces.

3 Return the stock to the saucepan and bring to the boil. Adjust the heat so the liquid boils very gently. Add the carrots, cover and cook for 5 minutes. Add the potatoes, cover again and cook for about 12 minutes, or until the vegetables are beginning to become tender.

4 Meanwhile, put the flour in a small mixing bowl and very gradually whisk in the milk to make a thick paste. Pour in a little of the hot stock mixture and stir well to make a smooth liquid.

5 Stir the flour mixture into the soup and bring just to the boil, stirring. Boil gently for 4–5 minutes, until it thickens, stirring frequently.

6 Add the spring onions, asparagus and chicken. Reduce the heat and simmer for about 15 minutes, until all the vegetables are tender. Stir in the cream and herbs. Season and serve.

spinach & ginger soup

serves four

2 tbsp sunflower oil

1 onion, chopped

2 garlic cloves,
    chopped finely

2 tsp finely chopped fresh
    root ginger

250 g/9 oz fresh young
    spinach leaves

1 small lemon grass stalk,
    chopped finely

1 litre/1¾ pints chicken or
    vegetable stock

225 g/8 oz potatoes, chopped

1 tbsp rice wine or
    dry sherry

1 tsp sesame oil

salt and pepper

1 Heat the oil in a large saucepan. Add the onion, garlic and ginger, and fry gently for 3–4 minutes, until softened but not browned.

2 Reserve 2–3 small spinach leaves. Add the remaining leaves and lemon grass to the saucepan, stirring until the spinach is wilted. Add the stock and potatoes to the pan and bring to the boil. Lower the heat, cover and simmer for about 10 minutes.

3 Tip the soup into a blender or food processor and process until completely smooth.

4 Return the soup to the pan and add the rice wine or sherry, then adjust the seasoning. Heat to just below boiling point.

5 Finely shred the 2–3 reserved spinach leaves and scatter some over the top. Drizzle with a few drops of sesame oil and serve the soup hot, garnished with the finely shredded fresh spinach leaves.

COOK'S TIP

To make a creamy-textured spinach and coconut soup, stir in about 4 tablespoons creamed coconut, or alternatively replace about 300 ml/10 fl oz of the stock with coconut milk. (Coconut milk is available in cans from supermarkets and Asian food stores.) Serve the soup with shavings of fresh coconut scattered over the surface.

potato & split pea soup

serves four

2 tbsp vegetable oil

450 g/1 lb unpeeled floury
    potatoes, diced

2 onions, diced

75 g/2¾ oz split green peas

1 litre/1¾ pints vegetable stock

60 g/2¼ oz Gruyère cheese, grated

salt and pepper

CROÛTONS

3 tbsp butter

1 garlic clove, crushed

1 tbsp chopped fresh parsley

1 thick slice white bread, diced

1 Heat the vegetable oil in a large saucepan. Add the potatoes and onions and sauté over a low heat, stirring constantly, for about 5 minutes.

2 Add the split green peas to the pan and stir together well.

3 Pour the vegetable stock into the pan and bring to the boil. Reduce the heat to low and simmer for about 35 minutes, until the potatoes are tender and the split peas are cooked.

4 Meanwhile, make the croûtons. Melt the butter in a frying pan. Add the garlic, parsley and bread cubes and cook, turning frequently, for about 2 minutes, until golden all over.

5 Stir the grated cheese into the soup and season to taste with salt and pepper. Heat gently until the cheese is starting to melt.

6 Pour the soup into warmed individual bowls and sprinkle the croûtons on top. Serve at once.

lentil, potato & ham soup

serves five

300 g/10½ oz Puy lentils

2 tsp butter

1 large onion, chopped finely

2 carrots, chopped finely

1 garlic clove, chopped finely

450 ml/16 fl oz water

1 bay leaf

¼ tsp dried sage or rosemary

1 litre/1¾ pints chicken or
      vegetable stock

225 g/8 oz potatoes, finely diced

1 tbsp tomato purée

115 g/4 oz smoked ham,
      diced finely

salt and pepper

chopped fresh parsley,
      to garnish

1 Rinse and drain the lentils and pick them over to remove any small stones if necessary.

2 Melt the butter in a large, heavy-based saucepan or flameproof casserole over a medium heat. Add the onion, carrots and garlic, cover and cook, stirring frequently, for about 4–5 minutes, until the onion is slightly softened but not browned.

3 Add the lentils to the vegetables with the measured water, bay leaf and sage or rosemary. Bring to the boil, reduce the heat, cover and simmer for 10 minutes.

4 Add the stock, potatoes, tomato purée and ham. Bring back to a simmer. Cover and continue simmering for 25–30 minutes, or until the vegetables are tender.

5 Season to taste with salt and pepper and remove the bay leaf. Ladle into warm bowls, garnish with parsley and serve.

broccoli & potato soup

serves four

2 tbsp olive oil

450 g/1 lb potatoes, diced

1 onion, diced

225 g/8 oz broccoli florets

125 g/4½ oz blue cheese, crumbled

1 litre/1¾ pints vegetable stock

150 m/5 fl oz double cream

paprika

salt and pepper

COOK'S TIP

This soup freezes very successfully. Follow the method described here up to step 4, and freeze the soup after it has been puréed. Add the cream and paprika just before serving. Garnish and serve.

VARIATION

This soup also tastes delicious made with grated mature Cheddar instead of blue cheese.

1 Heat the oil in a large saucepan. Add the potatoes and onion. Sauté, stirring constantly, for 5 minutes.

2 Reserve a few broccoli florets for the garnish and add the remaining broccoli to the pan. Add the cheese and vegetable stock.

3 Bring to the boil, then reduce the heat, cover the pan and simmer gently for about 25 minutes, until the potatoes are tender.

4 Transfer the soup to a food processor or blender, in batches, and process until the mixture is smooth. Alternatively, press the vegetables through a strainer with the back of a wooden spoon.

5 Return the purée to a clean saucepan and stir in the double cream and a pinch of paprika. Season to taste with salt and pepper.

6 Blanch the reserved broccoli florets in a little boiling water for about 2 minutes, then lift them out of the pan with a slotted spoon.

7 Pour the soup into warmed individual bowls and garnish with the broccoli florets and a sprinkling of paprika. Serve the soup immediately.

broad bean & mint soup

serves four

2 tbsp olive oil

1 red onion, chopped

2 garlic cloves, crushed

450 g/1 lb potatoes, diced

500 g/1 lb 2 oz broad beans,
    thawed if frozen

850 ml/1½ pints vegetable stock

2 tbsp freshly chopped mint

natural yogurt and fresh mint sprigs,
    to garnish

1 Heat the olive oil in a large saucepan. Add the onion and garlic and sauté for 2–3 minutes, until softened.

2 Add the potatoes and cook, stirring constantly, for 5 minutes.

3 Stir in the beans and the stock, then cover the pan and simmer for 30 minutes, or until the beans and potatoes are tender.

4 Remove a few vegetables with a slotted spoon and reserve. Place the remainder of the soup in a food processor or blender and process until smooth.

5 Return the soup to a clean saucepan and add the reserved vegetables and chopped mint. Stir thoroughly and heat through gently.

6 Transfer the soup to a warm tureen or individual serving bowls. Garnish with swirls of natural yogurt and sprigs of fresh mint and serve immediately.

roasted garlic & potato soup

serves four

1 large garlic bulb with large cloves,
    peeled (about 100 g/3½ oz)

2 tsp olive oil, plus extra
    for brushing

2 large leeks, sliced thinly

1 large onion, chopped finely

500 g/1 lb 2 oz potatoes, diced

1.2 litres/2 pints chicken or
    vegetable stock

1 bay leaf

150 ml/5 fl oz single cream

freshly grated nutmeg

fresh lemon juice (optional)

salt and pepper

TO GARNISH

snipped fresh chives

sprinkle of paprika

1 Put the garlic cloves in an ovenproof dish, lightly brush with oil and bake in a preheated oven, 180°C/350°F/Gas Mark 4 for about 20 minutes, until golden.

2 Heat the oil in a large saucepan over a medium heat. Add the leeks and onion, cover and cook for about 3 minutes, stirring frequently, until they begin to soften.

3 Add the potatoes, roasted garlic, stock and bay leaf. Season with salt (unless the stock is salty already) and pepper. Bring to the boil, reduce the heat, cover and cook gently for about 30 minutes, until the vegetables are tender. Remove the bay leaf.

4 Allow the soup to cool slightly, then transfer to a blender or food processor and process until smooth, working in batches if necessary. (If using a food processor, strain off the cooking liquid and reserve. Process the soup solids with enough cooking liquid to moisten them, then combine with the remaining liquid.)

5 Return the soup to the saucepan and stir in the cream and a generous grating of nutmeg. Taste and adjust the seasoning, if necessary, adding a few drops of lemon juice if desired. Reheat over a low heat. Ladle into warm soup bowls, garnish with chives and paprika and serve.

25

sweet potato & apple soup

serves six

1 tbsp butter

3 leeks, sliced thinly

1 large carrot, sliced thinly

600 g/1 lb 5 oz sweet potatoes,
  peeled and diced

2 large, tart eating apples, peeled
  and diced

l.2 litres/2 pints water

freshly grated nutmeg

225 ml/8 fl oz apple juice

225 ml/8 fl oz single cream, plus
  extra to garnish

salt and pepper

snipped fresh chives or chopped
  fresh coriander, to garnish

1 Melt the butter in a large saucepan over a medium–low heat. Add the leeks, cover and cook, stirring frequently, for 6–8 minutes, or until softened.

2 Add the carrot, sweet potatoes, apples and water. Season lightly with salt, pepper and nutmeg to taste. Bring to the boil, reduce the heat and cover and simmer, stirring occasionally, for about 20 minutes until the vegetables are very tender.

3 Allow the soup to cool slightly, then transfer to a blender or food processor and process until smooth, working in batches if necessary. (If using a food processor, strain off the cooking liquid and reserve. Process the soup solids with enough cooking liquid to moisten them, then combine with the remaining liquid.)

4 Return the puréed soup to the saucepan and stir in the apple juice. Place over a low heat and simmer for about 10 minutes, until heated through.

5 Stir in the cream and continue simmering for about 5 minutes, stirring frequently, until heated through. Taste and adjust the seasoning, adding more salt, pepper and nutmeg, if necessary.

6 Ladle into warm bowls, garnish with a swirl of cream, sprinkle with chives or coriander and serve.

celeriac, leek & potato soup

serves four

1 tbsp butter

1 onion, chopped

2 large leeks, halved lengthways
    and sliced

750 g/1 lb 10 oz celeriac, peeled
    and diced

225 g/8 oz potatoes, diced

1 carrot, quartered and sliced thinly

1.2 litres/2 pints water

pinch of dried marjoram

1 bay leaf

freshly grated nutmeg

salt and pepper

celery leaves, to garnish

1 Melt the butter in a large saucepan over a medium–low heat. Add the onion and leeks and cook for about 4 minutes, stirring frequently, until just softened and translucent but not coloured.

2 Add the celeriac, potatoes, carrot, water, marjoram and bay leaf, with a large pinch of salt. Bring to the boil, reduce the heat, cover and simmer for about 25 minutes, until the vegetables are tender. Remove the bay leaf.

3 Allow the soup to cool slightly. Transfer to a blender or food processor and process until smooth. (If using a food processor, strain off the cooking liquid and reserve. Process the soup solids with enough cooking liquid to moisten them, then combine with the remaining liquid.)

4 Return the puréed soup to the saucepan and stir to blend the ingredients thoroughly. Season the soup with nutmeg, salt and pepper to taste, then simmer over a medium–low heat until reheated.

5 Ladle the soup into warm bowls, garnish with celery leaves and then serve immediately.

vegetable & corn chowder

serves four

1 tbsp vegetable oil

1 red onion, diced

1 red pepper, deseeded and diced

3 garlic cloves, crushed

300 g/10½ oz potatoes, diced

2 tbsp plain flour

600 ml/1 pint milk

300 ml/10 fl oz vegetable stock

50 g/1¾ oz broccoli florets

300 g/10½ oz canned
    sweetcorn, drained

75 g/2¾ oz Cheddar cheese, grated

salt and pepper

1 tbsp chopped fresh coriander,
    to garnish

COOK'S TIP

Vegetarian cheeses are made
with rennets of non-animal
origin, using microbial or
fungal enzymes.

1 Heat the oil in a large, heavy-based saucepan. Add the onion, red pepper, garlic and diced potatoes and cook over a low heat, stirring frequently, for 2–3 minutes, until the onion is softened.

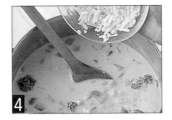

2 Stir in the flour and cook, stirring constantly, for 30 seconds. Gradually stir in the milk and vegetable stock until smooth.

3 Add the broccoli and sweetcorn. Bring the mixture to the boil, stirring constantly, then reduce the heat and simmer for about 20 minutes, or until all the vegetables are tender.

4 Stir in 50 g/1¾ oz of the cheese until it melts.

5 Season to taste with salt and pepper, then spoon the chowder into a warm soup tureen. Garnish with the remaining grated cheese and the coriander and serve immediately.

green soup

serves four

1 tbsp olive oil

1 onion, chopped

1 garlic clove, chopped

200 g/7 oz potato, cut into
  2.5-cm/1-inch cubes

700 ml/1¼ pints vegetable or
  chicken stock

1 small cucumber or ½ large
  cucumber, cut into chunks

85 g/3 oz watercress

125 g/4½ oz green beans, trimmed
  and halved lengthways

salt and pepper

VARIATION
Try using 125 g/4½ oz
mangetouts instead
of the beans.

COOK'S TIP
The most suitable olive oil for
cooking is virgin oil. 'Pure' oil is
highly refined and likely to have
been heat treated.

1 Heat the oil in a large pan and cook the onion and garlic over a medium heat, stirring occasionally, for 3–4 minutes, or until softened.

2 Add the potato cubes and cook for a further 2–3 minutes. Stir in the vegetable or chicken stock and bring to the boil. Lower the heat and simmer for 5 minutes.

3 Add the cucumber to the pan and cook for a further 3 minutes or until the potatoes are tender. Test by inserting the tip of a sharp knife into the potato cubes – it should pass through easily.

4 Add the watercress and cook until just wilted. Remove from heat and leave to cool slightly, then transfer to a food processor and process to a smooth purée. Alternatively, before adding the watercress, mash the vegetables with a potato masher and push through a sieve, then chop the watercress finely and stir into the soup.

5 Bring a small pan of water to the boil and steam the beans for 3–4 minutes, or until tender. Add the beans to the soup, season to taste with salt and pepper and warm through. Ladle into warmed soup bowls and serve immediately or leave to cool and then chill.

carrot & cumin soup

serves four-six

3 tbsp butter or margarine

1 large onion, chopped

1–2 garlic cloves, crushed

350 g/12 oz carrots, sliced

850 ml/1½ pints chicken or
   vegetable stock

¾ tsp ground cumin

2 celery sticks, sliced thinly

115 g/4 oz potato, diced

2 tsp tomato purée

2 tsp lemon juice

2 fresh or dried bay leaves

about 300 ml/ 10 fl oz
   skimmed milk

salt and pepper

celery leaves, to garnish

1 Melt the butter or margarine in a large pan. Add the onion and garlic and cook over a low heat, stirring occasionally, until softened.

2 Add the sliced carrots and cook gently for a further 5 minutes, stirring frequently and taking care they do not brown.

3 Add the stock, cumin, celery, potato, tomato purée, lemon juice and bay leaves, season to taste with salt and pepper and bring to the boil. Cover and simmer for about 30 minutes until the vegetables are tender.

4 Remove and discard the bay leaves, leave the soup to cool a little and then press it through a sieve or process in a food processor or blender until smooth.

5 Pour the soup into a clean pan, add the milk and bring to the boil over a low heat. Taste and adjust the seasoning if necessary.

6 Ladle into warmed bowls, garnish each serving with a small celery leaf and serve.

COOK'S TIP
This soup can be frozen for
up to 3 months. Add the milk
when reheating.

sweet potato & squash soup

serves six

350 g/12 oz sweet potatoes

1 acorn squash

4 shallots

olive oil, for brushing

5–6 garlic cloves, unpeeled

850 ml/1½ pints chicken stock

125 ml/4 fl oz single cream

salt and pepper

snipped fresh chives, to garnish

1 Cut the sweet potatoes, squash and shallots in half lengthways. Brush the cut sides with oil.

2 Put the vegetables, cut sides down, in a shallow roasting tin. Add the garlic cloves. Roast in a preheated oven, 190°C/375°F/Gas Mark 5, for about 40 minutes, until tender and light brown.

3 When cool, scoop the flesh from the potato and squash halves and put in a saucepan with the shallots. Squeeze out the soft insides from the garlic and add to the other vegetables.

4 Add the stock and a pinch of salt. Bring just to the boil, reduce the heat and simmer, partially covered, for about 30 minutes, stirring occasionally, until the vegetables are very tender.

5 Allow the soup to cool slightly, then process in a blender or food processor until smooth, in batches if necessary. (If using a food processor, strain off the cooking liquid and reserve. Process the soup solids with enough cooking liquid to moisten them, then combine with the liquid.)

6 Return the soup to the pan and stir in the cream. Season, then simmer for 5–10 minutes, until heated through and serve immediately.

watercress vichyssoise

serves six

1 tbsp olive oil

3 large leeks, sliced thinly

350 g/12 oz potatoes, diced finely

600 ml/1 pint chicken or
   vegetable stock

450 ml/16 fl oz water

1 bay leaf

175 g/6 oz prepared watercress

175 ml/6 fl oz single cream

salt and pepper

watercress leaves, to garnish

1 Heat the oil in a heavy-based saucepan over a medium heat. Add the sliced leeks and cook for about 3 minutes, stirring frequently, until they begin to soften.

COOK'S TIP

For garlic croûtons, cut off the crusts from 3 slices of day-old bread, then cut the bread into 5-mm/¼-inch dice. Heat 3 tablespoons olive oil in a frying pan and stir-fry 1 chopped large garlic clove for 2 minutes, then remove. Fry the diced bread until golden all over. Drain well.

2 Add the potatoes, stock, water and bay leaf. Add salt if the stock is unsalted. Bring to the boil, then reduce the heat, cover the saucepan and cook gently for about 25 minutes, until the vegetables are tender. Remove the bay leaf and discard it.

3 Add the watercress and continue to cook, stirring frequently, for a further 2–3 minutes, until the watercress is completely wilted.

4 Allow the soup to cool slightly, then transfer to a blender or food processor and process until smooth, working in batches if necessary. (If using a food processor, strain off the cooking liquid and reserve. Process the soup solids with enough cooking liquid to moisten them, then combine with the remaining liquid.)

5 Put the soup into a large bowl and then stir in half the cream. Season with salt, if needed, and plenty of pepper. Leave to cool to room temperature.

6 Chill in the refrigerator until cold. Taste and adjust the seasoning, if necessary. Ladle into chilled bowls, drizzle the remaining cream on top and garnish with watercress leaves. Serve the soup immediately.

minted pea & yogurt soup

serves six

2 tbsp vegetable ghee or
   sunflower oil

2 onions, chopped coarsely

225 g/8 oz potato, chopped
   coarsely

2 garlic cloves

2.5-cm/1-inch piece of root
   ginger, chopped

1 tsp ground coriander

1 tsp ground cumin

1 tbsp plain flour

850 ml/1½ pints vegetable stock

500 g/1 lb 2 oz frozen peas

2–3 tbsp chopped fresh mint

150 ml/5 fl oz Greek-style yogurt,
   plus extra to garnish

½ tsp cornflour

300 ml/10 fl oz milk

salt and pepper

fresh mint sprigs, to garnish

2 Stir in the garlic, ginger, coriander, cumin and flour and cook, stirring constantly, for 1 minute.

3 Add the vegetable stock, peas and half the mint and bring to the boil, stirring constantly. Reduce the heat to very low, cover and simmer gently for 15 minutes, or until the vegetables are tender.

4 Process the soup, in batches, in a blender or food processor. Return the mixture to the pan and season with salt and pepper to taste. Blend the yogurt with the cornflour to a smooth paste and stir into the soup.

1 Heat the vegetable ghee or sunflower oil in a saucepan, add the onions and potato and cook over a low heat, stirring occasionally, for about 3 minutes, until the onion is soft and translucent.

5 Add the milk and bring almost to the boil, stirring constantly. Cook very gently for 2 minutes. Serve hot, garnished with small fresh mint sprigs and a swirl of extra yogurt.

vichyssoise

serves six

3 large leeks

3 tbsp butter or margarine

1 onion, sliced thinly

500 g/1 lb 2 oz potatoes, chopped

850 ml/1½ pints vegetable stock

2 tsp lemon juice

pinch of ground nutmeg

¼ tsp ground coriander

1 bay leaf

1 egg yolk

150 ml/5 fl oz single cream

salt and pepper

snipped fresh chives, to garnish

1 Trim the leeks and remove most of the green parts. Slice the white parts of the leeks very thinly.

2 Melt the butter or margarine in a large, heavy-based saucepan. Add the leeks and onion and fry over a medium heat, stirring occasionally, for about 5 minutes without browning.

3 Add the potatoes, vegetable stock, lemon juice, nutmeg, coriander and bay leaf to the pan, season to taste with salt and pepper and bring to the boil. Cover and simmer for about 30 minutes, until all the vegetables are very soft.

4 Cool the soup a little, remove and discard the bay leaf and then press through a sieve or process in a food processor or blender until smooth. Pour into a clean pan.

5 Blend the egg yolk into the cream, add a little of the soup to the mixture and then whisk it all back into the soup and reheat gently, without boiling. Adjust the seasoning to taste. Leave to cool and then chill thoroughly in the refrigerator.

6 Serve the soup sprinkled with snipped fresh chives.

fennel & tomato soup

serves four

2 tsp olive oil

1 large onion, halved and sliced

2 large fennel bulbs, halved
and sliced

1 small potato, diced

850 ml/1½ pints water

400 ml/14 fl oz tomato juice

1 bay leaf

125 g/4½ oz cooked peeled
small prawns

2 tomatoes, skinned, deseeded
and chopped

½ tsp chopped fresh dill

salt and pepper

fresh dill sprigs or fennel fronds,
to garnish

COOK'S TIP

When buying fennel, look for
well-rounded, plump bulbs with
no signs of bruising or
discoloration. The bulbs should
be dry, but not dried out.

1 Heat the olive oil in a large
saucepan over a medium heat.
Add the sliced onion and fennel and
cook stirring occasionally, for about
3–4 minutes, until the onion is just
softened but not coloured.

2 Add the potato, water, tomato
juice and bay leaf with a large
pinch of salt. Reduce the heat, cover
and simmer for about 25 minutes,
stirring once or twice, until the
vegetables are soft.

3 Allow the soup to cool slightly,
then transfer to a blender or food
processor and process until smooth,
working in batches if necessary. (If
using a food processor, strain off the
cooking liquid and reserve. Process the
soup solids with enough cooking liquid
to moisten them, then combine with
the remaining liquid.)

4 Return the soup to a clean
saucepan and stir in the prawns.
Simmer gently over a low heat for
about 10 minutes, to reheat the soup
and allow it to absorb the prawn
flavour fully.

5 Stir in the tomatoes and dill. Taste
and adjust the seasoning, adding
salt, if needed, and pepper. Thin the
soup with a little more tomato juice,
if wished. Ladle into warm bowls,
garnish with dill sprigs or fennel fronds
and serve.

new england clam chowder

serves four

900 g/2 lb live clams

4 rindless streaky bacon
rashers, chopped

2 tbsp butter

1 onion, chopped

1 tbsp chopped fresh thyme

300 g/10½ oz potatoes, diced

300 ml/10 fl oz milk

1 bay leaf

150 ml/5 fl oz double cream

1 tbsp chopped fresh parsley

salt and pepper

fresh thyme sprigs to garnish

1 Scrub the clams and put into a large saucepan with a splash of water. Cook over a high heat for 3–4 minutes, until all the clams have opened. Discard any that remain closed. Strain the clams, reserving the cooking liquid. Leave until cool enough to handle.

2 Reserve 8 clams for the garnish. Remove the remainder from their shells, chop if large and reserve.

3 In a clean saucepan, fry the bacon until browned and crisp. Drain on kitchen paper. Add the butter to the same pan and when it has melted, add the onion. Cook for

4–5 minutes, until softened but not coloured. Add the thyme and cook briefly before adding the diced potatoes, reserved clam cooking liquid, milk and bay leaf. Bring to the boil and simmer for 10 minutes until the potatoes are tender but not falling apart. Remove the bay leaf.

4 Transfer to a food processor and process until smooth or push through a sieve into a bowl.

5 Add the reserved clams, the bacon and the cream. Simmer for an additional 2–3 minutes, until heated through. Season, then stir in the parsley, garnish and serve.

smoked haddock soup

serves four

1 tbsp vegetable oil

55 g/2 oz smoked streaky bacon,
    cut into matchsticks

1 large onion, chopped finely

2 tbsp plain flour

1 litre/1¾ pints milk

700 g/1 lb 9 oz potatoes, diced

175 g/6 oz skinless smoked
    haddock fillet

salt and pepper

finely chopped fresh parsley, to
    garnish

COOK'S TIP

Cutting the potatoes into small
cubes not only looks attractive,
it allows them to cook more
quickly and evenly.

1 Heat the oil in a large saucepan over a medium heat. Add the bacon and cook for 2 minutes. Stir in the onion and continue cooking for 5–7 minutes, stirring frequently, until the onion is soft and the bacon golden. Tip the pan and spoon off as much fat as possible.

2 Stir in the flour and continue cooking for 2 minutes. Add half of the milk and stir well, scraping the bottom of the pan to mix in the flour.

3 Add the potatoes and remaining milk and season with pepper. Bring just to the boil, stirring frequently, then reduce the heat and simmer gently, partially covered, for 10 minutes.

4 Add the fish and continue cooking, stirring occasionally, for about 15 minutes, or until the potatoes are tender and the fish breaks up easily.

5 Taste the soup and adjust the seasoning if necessary (salt may not be needed). Ladle into a warm tureen or soup bowls and sprinkle generously with chopped parsley.

41

bouillabaisse

serves six

450 g/1 lb large raw prawns

750 g/1 lb 10 oz firm white fish
fillets, such as sea bass, snapper
and monkfish

4 tbsp olive oil

grated rind of 1 orange

1 large garlic clove, chopped finely

½ tsp chilli paste or harissa

1 large leek, sliced

1 onion, halved and sliced

1 red pepper, deseeded and sliced

3–4 tomatoes, cored and cut
into eighths

4 garlic cloves, sliced

1 bay leaf

pinch of saffron threads

½ tsp fennel seeds

600 ml/1 pint water

1.2 litres/2 pints fish stock

1 fennel bulb, chopped finely

1 large onion, chopped finely

225 g/8 oz potatoes, halved and
sliced thinly

250 g/9 oz scallops

salt and pepper

TO SERVE

ready-prepared aïoli

toasted French bread slices

fresh dill sprigs to garnish

1 Peel the prawns and reserve the shells. Cut the fish fillets into serving pieces about 5-cm/2-inch square. Trim off any ragged edges and reserve. Put the fish in a bowl with 2 tablespoons of the olive oil, the orange rind, garlic and chilli paste or harissa. Turn to coat well, cover and chill the prawns and fish separately.

2 Heat 1 tablespoon of the remaining olive oil in a large saucepan over a medium heat. Add the leek, sliced onion and red pepper. Cook, stirring constantly, for 5 minutes, until the onion softens.

3 Stir in the tomatoes, sliced garlic, bay leaf, saffron, fennel seeds, prawn shells, water and fish stock. Bring to the boil, then simmer, covered, for 30 minutes. Strain the stock.

4 Heat the remaining oil in a large pan. Add the fennel and chopped onion and cook, stirring, for 5 minutes, until softened. Add the stock and potatoes and bring to the boil. Reduce the heat slightly, cover and cook for 12–15 minutes, until just tender.

5 Lower the heat and add the chilled fish, starting with thick pieces and adding thinner ones after 2–3 minutes. Add the chilled prawns and scallops and continue simmering gently until all the seafood is cooked and opaque throughout.

6 Taste the soup and adjust the seasoning. Ladle into warm bowls. Spread the aïoli sauce on the toasted bread slices and arrange on top of the soup. Garnish and serve.

COOK'S TIP

There are as many versions of bouillabaisse as there are villages on the French Mediterranean coast. You can use whatever fish you like, but it is best to choose thick fillets with firm flesh.

Salads, Starters & Light Meals

Potatoes are very versatile and can be used as a base to create an array of tempting light meals. They are very nutritious, and their carbohydrate content gives a welcome energy boost. Potatoes have a neutral flavour, and can be teamed with a variety of other ingredients and flavours.

Also featured in this chapter are starters and salads based on potatoes. In addition to the creamy potato salads that are so popular, there are many other recipes to tempt your palate, including dishes suitable for light lunches. Many are also ideal for barbecues and picnics.

nests of chinese salad

serves four

POTATO NESTS

450 g/1 lb floury potatoes, grated

125 g/4½ oz cornflour

vegetable oil, for frying

fresh chives, to garnish

SALAD

125 g/4½ oz pineapple, diced

1 green pepper, deseeded and cut
   into strips

1 carrot, cut into matchsticks

50 g/1¾ oz mangetout,
   thickly sliced

4 baby sweetcorn cobs,
   halved lengthways

25 g/1 oz beansprouts

2 spring onions, sliced

DRESSING

1 tbsp clear honey

1 tsp light soy sauce

1 garlic clove, crushed

1 tsp lemon juice

COOK'S TIP

A wok is ideal for cooking the
nests, but you could use a large,
heavy-based frying pan.

1 To make the nests, rinse the grated potato several times in cold water. Drain well on kitchen paper to dry the potato completely This is to prevent the nests from spitting when they are cooked in the oil. Place the potato in a mixing bowl. Add the cornflour, mixing well to thoroughly coat the potato.

2 Half fill a wok with vegetable oil and heat until smoking. Line a 15-cm/6-inch diameter wire sieve with a quarter of the potato mixture and press another sieve of the same size on top.

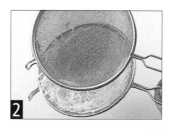

3 Lower the sieves into the oil and cook for 2 minutes, until the potato nest is golden brown and crisp. Remove from the wok, and drain thoroughly on kitchen paper.

4 Repeat 3 more times to use up all of the mixture and make a total of 4 nests. Leave to cool.

5 Mix the salad ingredients together, then spoon into the potato baskets.

6 To make the dressing, mix all of the dressing ingredients together. Pour the dressing over the salad, garnish with chives and serve immediately.

beetroot salad & dill dressing

serves four

450 g/1 lb waxy potatoes, diced

4 small cooked beetroot, sliced

½ small cucumber, sliced thinly

2 large dill pickles, sliced

1 red onion, halved and sliced

fresh dill sprigs, to garnish

DRESSING

1 garlic clove, crushed

2 tbsp olive oil

2 tbsp red wine vinegar

2 tbsp chopped fresh dill

salt and pepper

1 Cook the potatoes in a saucepan of boiling water for 15 minutes, or until tender. Drain and leave to cool.

2 When cool, mix the potatoes and beetroot together in a bowl, cover with clingfilm and reserve.

3 Line a salad platter with the slices of cucumber, dill pickles and red onion.

4 Spoon the potato and beetroot mixture into the centre of the salad platter.

5 In a small bowl, whisk all the dressing ingredients together, then pour the dressing over the salad.

6 Serve the potato and beetroot salad immediately, garnished with fresh dill sprigs.

grilled new potato salad

serves four

650 g/1 lb 7 oz new
  potatoes, scrubbed

3 tbsp olive oil

2 tbsp chopped fresh thyme

1 tsp paprika

4 smoked bacon rashers

salt and pepper

fresh parsley sprig, to garnish

DRESSING

4 tbsp mayonnaise

1 tbsp garlic wine vinegar

2 garlic cloves, crushed

1 tbsp chopped fresh parsley

1 Cook the new potatoes in a saucepan of boiling water for 10 minutes. Drain thoroughly.

2 Mix the olive oil, thyme and paprika together and pour the mixture over the warm potatoes.

3 Place the bacon rashers under a preheated medium grill and cook, turning once, for 5 minutes, until crisp. When cooked, roughly chop the bacon and keep warm.

4 Transfer the potatoes to the grill pan and cook for 10 minutes, turning once.

5 Mix the dressing ingredients in a small serving bowl. Transfer the potatoes and bacon to a large serving bowl. Season with salt and pepper and mix together.

6 Spoon over the dressing, garnish with a parsley sprig and serve immediately if you are serving the salad warm. Alternatively, leave to cool and serve chilled.

indian potato salad

serves four

900 g/2 lb floury potatoes, diced

75 g/2¾ oz small broccoli florets

1 small mango, diced

4 spring onions, sliced

salt and pepper

small cooked spiced poppadoms,
    to serve

DRESSING

½ tsp ground cumin

½ tsp ground coriander

1 tbsp mango chutney

150 ml/5 fl oz low-fat natural yogurt

1 tsp chopped fresh root ginger

2 tbsp chopped fresh coriander

1 Cook the potatoes in a saucepan of boiling water for 10 minutes, or until tender. Drain and place in a mixing bowl.

2 Meanwhile, blanch the broccoli florets in a separate saucepan of boiling water for 2 minutes. Drain the broccoli well and add the florets to the potatoes in the bowl.

3 When the potatoes and broccoli have cooled, add the mango and spring onions. Season to taste with salt and pepper and mix well to combine.

4 In a small bowl, stir all of the dressing ingredients together.

5 Spoon the dressing over the potato mixture and mix together carefully, taking care not to break up the potatoes and broccoli.

6 Serve the salad immediately, accompanied by the small cooked spiced poppadoms.

mexican potato salad

serves four

1.25 kg/2 lb 12 oz waxy
  · potatoes, sliced

1 ripe avocado

1 tsp olive oil

1 tsp lemon juice

1 garlic clove, crushed

1 onion, chopped

2 large tomatoes, sliced

1 fresh green chilli, deseeded
  and chopped

1 yellow pepper, deseeded and
  sliced

2 tbsp chopped fresh coriander

salt and pepper

lemon or lime wedges, to garnish

3 Add the olive oil, lemon juice,
garlic and onion to the avocado
flesh and stir to mix. Cover the bowl
with clingfilm, to minimize
discoloration, and reserve.

4 Mix the tomatoes, chilli and
yellow pepper together and
transfer to a salad bowl with the
potato slices.

5 Arrange the avocado mixture on
top of the salad and sprinkle with
the chopped coriander. Season to taste
with salt and pepper and serve
immediately, garnished with lemon or
lime wedges.

1 Cook the potato slices in a
saucepan of boiling water for
10–15 minutes, or until tender.
Drain and leave to cool.

2 Meanwhile, cut the avocado
in half, remove the stone and
peel. Mash the avocado flesh with a
fork (you could also scoop the avocado
flesh from the 2 halves using a
spoon and then mash it).

sweet potato salad

serves four

500 g/1 lb 2 oz sweet
   potatoes, diced

4 tbsp butter

1 tbsp lemon juice

1 garlic clove, crushed

1 red pepper, deseeded and diced

1 green pepper, deseeded and diced

2 bananas, sliced thickly

2 thick slices white bread, crusts
   removed, diced

salt and pepper

DRESSING

2 tbsp clear honey

2 tbsp snipped fresh chives

2 tbsp lemon juice

2 tbsp olive oil

COOK'S TIP

Use firm, slightly underripe
bananas in this recipe because
they won't turn soft and mushy
when they are fried.

1 Cook the sweet potatoes in a saucepan of boiling water for 10–15 minutes, until tender. Drain thoroughly and reserve.

2 Meanwhile, melt the butter in a frying pan. Add the lemon juice, garlic and peppers and cook, stirring constantly for 3 minutes.

3 Add the banana slices to the pan and cook for 1 minute. Remove the bananas from the pan with a slotted spoon and stir into the potatoes.

4 Add the bread cubes to the frying pan and cook, stirring frequently, for 2 minutes, until they are golden brown on all sides.

5 Mix the dressing ingredients together in a small saucepan and heat until thoroughly blended.

6 Spoon the potato mixture into a serving dish and season to taste with salt and pepper. Pour the dressing over the potatoes and sprinkle the croûtons over the top. Serve the sweet potato salad immediately.

potato salad

serves four

700 g/1 lb 9 oz tiny new potatoes

8 spring onions

1 hard-boiled egg (optional)

250 ml/9 fl oz low-fat mayonnaise

1 tsp paprika

salt and pepper

TO GARNISH

2 tbsp snipped fresh chives

pinch of paprika

COOK'S TIP

To make a lighter dressing, use a mixture of half mayonnaise and half natural yogurt.

1 Bring a large pan of lightly salted water to the boil. Add the new potatoes to the pan and cook for 10–15 minutes, or until they are just tender.

2 Drain the potatoes in a colander and rinse them under cold running water until they are completely cold. Drain them again thoroughly. Transfer the potatoes to a mixing bowl and leave until required.

3 Trim and slice the spring onions thinly on the diagonal. Chop the hard-boiled egg, if using.

4 Mix together the mayonnaise, paprika, and salt and pepper to taste in a bowl until well blended. Pour the mixture over the potatoes.

5 Add the sliced spring onions and egg, if using, to the potatoes and toss together.

6 Transfer the potato salad to a serving bowl, sprinkle with snipped chives and a pinch of paprika. Cover with clingfilm and chill in the refrigerator until required.

radish & cucumber salad

serves four

500 g/1 lb 2 oz new potatoes,
   scrubbed and halved

½ cucumber, sliced thinly

2 tsp salt

1 bunch of radishes, sliced thinly

DRESSING

1 tbsp Dijon mustard

2 tbsp olive oil

1 tbsp white wine vinegar

2 tbsp chopped mixed fresh herbs

1 Cook the potatoes in a large saucepan of boiling water for 10–15 minutes, or until tender. Drain and leave to cool.

2 Meanwhile, spread out the cucumber slices on a plate and sprinkle with the salt. Leave to stand for 30 minutes, then rinse thoroughly under cold running water and pat dry with kitchen paper.

3 Arrange the cucumber and radish slices on a serving plate in a decorative pattern and pile the cooked potatoes in the centre of the slices.

4 In a small bowl, mix all the dressing ingredients together, whisking until thoroughly combined. Pour the dressing over the salad. Cover the salad with clingfilm and chill in the refrigerator before serving.

COOK'S TIP

The cucumber adds not only colour but also a real freshness to the salad. It is salted and left to stand to remove the excess water, which would make the salad soggy. Wash the cucumber well to remove all of the salt before adding to the salad.

tuna niçoise salad

serves four

4 eggs

450 g/1 lb new potatoes

115 g/4 oz French green beans,
    trimmed and halved

2 x 175 g/6 oz tuna steaks

6 tbsp olive oil, plus extra
    for brushing

1 garlic clove, crushed

1½ tsp Dijon mustard

2 tsp lemon juice

2 tbsp chopped fresh basil

2 little gem lettuces

200 g/7 oz cherry tomatoes, halved

175 g/6 oz cucumber, peeled, cut in
    half and sliced

50 g/1¾ oz stoned black olives

50 g/1¾ oz canned anchovies in
    oil, drained

salt and pepper

1 Bring a small saucepan of water to the boil. Add the eggs and cook for 7–9 minutes from when the water returns to a boil: 7 minutes for a slightly soft centre, or 9 minutes for a firm centre. Drain and refresh under cold running water. Reserve.

2 Cook the potatoes in boiling salted water for 10–12 minutes, until tender. Add the beans 3 minutes before the end of the cooking time. Drain both vegetables well and refresh under cold water. Drain well.

3 Wash and dry the tuna steaks. Brush with a little olive oil and season. Cook on a preheated ridged griddle pan for 2–3 minutes each side, until just tender but still slightly pink in the centre. Leave to rest.

4 Whisk together the garlic, mustard, lemon juice, basil and seasoning. Whisk in the olive oil.

5 To assemble the salad, break apart the lettuces and tear into large pieces. Divide between individual serving plates. Next add the potatoes and beans, tomatoes, cucumber and olives. Toss lightly together. Shell the eggs and cut into quarters lengthwise. Arrange these on top of the salad. Scatter over the anchovies.

6 Flake the tuna steaks and arrange on the salad. Pour over the dressing and serve.

mixed vegetable salad

serves four

450 g/1 lb waxy new
   potatoes, scrubbed
1 carrot, cut into matchsticks
225 g/8 oz cauliflower florets
225 g/8 oz baby corn cobs,
   halved lengthways
175 g/6 oz green beans
175 g/6 oz ham, diced
50 g/1¾ oz mushrooms, sliced
salt and pepper
DRESSING
2 tbsp chopped fresh parsley
150 ml/5 fl oz mayonnaise
150 ml/5 fl oz natural yogurt
4 tsp lemon juice
grated rind of 1 lemon
2 tsp fennel seeds

1 Cook the potatoes in a pan of boiling water for 15 minutes, or until tender. Drain thoroughly and leave to cool. When the potatoes are cold, slice them thinly.

2 Meanwhile, cook the carrot matchsticks, cauliflower florets, baby corn cobs and green beans in a pan of boiling water for 5 minutes. Drain well and leave to cool.

COOK'S TIP

For a really quick salad, use a packet of frozen mixed vegetables, thawed, instead of fresh vegetables.

3 Reserving 1 teaspoon of the chopped parsley for the garnish, mix the remaining dressing ingredients together in a bowl. Season to taste.

4 Arrange the vegetables on a platter and top with the ham and mushrooms.

5 Spoon the dressing over the the salad and garnish with the reserved parsley. Serve at once.

lobster salad & lime dressing

serves four

450 g/1 lb waxy potatoes, scrubbed
and sliced

225 g/8 oz cooked lobster meat

150 ml/5 fl oz mayonnaise

2 tbsp lime juice

finely grated rind of 1 lime

1 tbsp chopped fresh parsley

2 tbsp olive oil

2 tomatoes, deseeded and diced

2 hard-boiled eggs, quartered

1 tbsp quartered stoned
green olives

salt and pepper

COOK'S TIP

As shellfish is used in this salad,
serve it immediately, or keep
covered and chilled for up to
1 hour before serving.

1 Cook the potatoes in a large saucepan of boiling water for 10–15 minutes, or until they are cooked through. Drain and reserve.

2 Remove the lobster meat from the shell and then separate it into large pieces.

3 In a bowl, mix together the mayonnaise, 1 tablespoon of the lime juice, half the grated lime rind and half the chopped parsley, amd reserve.

4 In a separate bowl, whisk the remaining lime juice with the olive oil and pour the dressing over the potatoes. Arrange the potatoes on a serving plate.

5 Top with the lobster meat, tomatoes, eggs and olives. Season with salt and pepper to taste and sprinkle with the reserved parsley.

6 Spoon the mayonnaise on to the centre of the salad, top with the reserved rind and serve.

spicy chicken salad

serves four

2 skinless, boneless chicken
   breast portions, about 125 g/
   4½ oz each

2 tbsp butter

1 fresh red chilli, deseeded
   and chopped

1 tbsp clear honey

½ tsp ground cumin

2 tbsp chopped fresh coriander

600 g/1 lb 5 oz potatoes, diced

50 g/1¾ oz green beans, halved

1 red pepper, deseeded and cut into
   thin strips

2 tomatoes, deseeded and diced

DRESSING

2 tbsp olive oil

pinch of chilli powder

1 tbsp garlic wine vinegar

pinch of caster sugar

1 tbsp chopped fresh coriander

1 Cut the chicken into thin strips. Melt the butter in a pan over a medium heat and add the chicken, chilli, honey and cumin. Cook for 10 minutes, turning until cooked through.

2 Transfer the mixture to a bowl, leave to cool, then stir in the chopped coriander.

3 Meanwhile, cook the diced potatoes in a saucepan of boiling water for 10 minutes, until tender. Drain well and leave to cool.

VARIATION

If you prefer, use lean turkey meat instead of the chicken for a slightly stronger taste. Use the white meat for the best appearance and flavour.

4 Blanch the green beans in boiling water for 3 minutes, then drain thoroughly and leave to cool. Mix the green beans and potatoes together in a large bowl.

5 Add the pepper and tomatoes to the potatoes and beans. Stir in the spicy chicken mixture.

6 In a small bowl, whisk together all the dressing ingredients and then pour the dressing over the salad, tossing well. Transfer to a salad bowl or large platter and serve immediately.

indonesian chicken salad

serves four

1.25 k/2 lb 12 oz waxy potatoes

300 g/10½ oz fresh pineapple,
   peeled and diced

2 carrots, grated

175 g/6 oz beansprouts

1 bunch of spring onions, sliced

1 large courgette, cut
   into matchsticks

3 celery sticks, cut into matchsticks

175 g/6 oz unsalted peanuts

2 cooked, skinless, boneless
   chicken breast portions, about
   125 g/4½ oz each, sliced

DRESSING

6 tbsp crunchy peanut butter

6 tbsp olive oil

2 tbsp light soy sauce

1 fresh red chilli, deseeded
   and chopped

2 tsp sesame oil

4 tsp lime juice

1 Using a sharp knife, cut the potatoes into small cubes. Bring a saucepan of water to the boil.

2 Cook the diced potatoes the pan of boiling water for 10 minutes, or until tender.

3 Drain the potatoes and leave to cool until required. When cool, transfer the potatoes to a salad bowl.

4 Add the pineapple, carrots, beansprouts, spring onions, courgette, celery, unsalted peanuts and sliced, cooked chicken to the potatoes. Toss thoroughly to mix all the salad ingredients together.

5 To make the dressing, put the peanut butter in a small mixing bowl and gradually whisk in the olive oil and light soy sauce, using a fork or a balloon whisk.

6 Stir in the chopped red chilli, sesame oil and lime juice. Mix until well combined.

7 Pour the spicy dressing over the salad and toss lightly to coat all of the ingredients. Serve the potato and chicken salad immediately.

italian sausage salad

serves four

450 g/1 lb waxy potatoes

1 radicchio or lollo rosso lettuce

1 green pepper, deseeded
and sliced

175 g/6 oz Italian sausage, sliced

1 red onion, halved and sliced

125 g/4½ oz sun-dried tomatoes in
oil, drained and sliced

2 tbsp shredded fresh basil

DRESSING

1 tbsp balsamic vinegar

1 tsp tomato purée

2 tbsp olive oil

salt and pepper

1 Cook the potatoes in a saucepan
of boiling water for 20 minutes,
or until cooked through. Drain and
leave to cool.

2 Wash the radicchio or lollo rosso
leaves and pat dry with kitchen
paper. Line a large serving platter with
the salad leaves.

3 Slice the cooled potatoes and
arrange them in layers on the
leaf-lined serving platter together with
the sliced green pepper, sliced Italian
sausage, red onion, sun-dried
tomatoes and shredded fresh basil.

4 Put the balsamic vinegar, tomato
purée and olive oil in a small
bowl, then whisk together until
thoroughly combined. Season to taste
with salt and pepper. Pour the dressing
over the potato salad and serve.

COOK'S TIP

Any sliced Italian sausage or
salami can be used in this salad.

potato, rocket & apple salad

serves four

600 g/1 lb 5 oz potatoes, unpeeled
and sliced

2 green eating apples, cored and
diced

1 tsp lemon juice

25 g/1 oz walnut pieces

125 g/4½ oz goat's cheese, diced

150 g/5½ oz rocket leaves

salt and pepper

DRESSING

2 tbsp olive oil

1 tbsp red wine vinegar

1 tsp clear honey

1 tsp fennel seeds

COOK'S TIP

Serve this salad immediately you
have finished preparing it
to prevent the apple from turning
unattractively brown.
Alternatively, prepare all of the
other ingredients in advance,
then dice and add the apple at
the last minute.

1 Cook the potatoes in a large pan
of boiling water for 15 minutes
until tender. Drain and leave to cool.
Transfer the cooled potatoes to a
serving bowl.

2 Toss the diced apples in the
lemon juice, then drain and stir
them into the cold potatoes.

3 Add the walnut pieces, cheese
cubes and rocket leaves, then toss
the ingredients together to mix.

4 In a small bowl or jug, whisk all
of the dressing ingredients
together and then pour the dressing
over the salad. Season to taste and
serve immediately.

spicy sweet potato slices

serves four

450 g/1 lb sweet potatoes

2 tbsp sunflower oil

1 tsp chilli sauce

salt and pepper

COOK'S TIP

For a simple spicy dip combine 150 ml/5 fl oz soured cream or Greek-style yogurt with ½ teaspoon sugar, ½ teaspoon Dijon mustard and salt and pepper to taste. Chill in the refrigerator until required.

1 Bring a large pan of water to the boil, add the unpeeled sweet potatoes and parboil them for about 10 minutes. Drain the sweet potatoes thoroughly and transfer to a chopping board. Leave to cool slightly.

2 Peel the potatoes and cut them into thick slices.

3 Mix together the sunflower oil, chilli sauce and salt and pepper to taste in a small bowl.

4 Brush the spicy mixture liberally over one side of the potatoes. Place the potatoes, oil side down, over medium hot coals on a barbecue and grill for 5–6 minutes.

5 Lightly brush the tops of the potatoes with the spice mixture, turn them over and cook for a further 5 minutes, or until crisp and golden.

6 Transfer the potatoes to a warm serving dish and serve at once.

potato kibbeh

serves four

175 g/6 oz bulgur wheat

350 g/12 oz floury potatoes, diced

2 small eggs, lightly beaten

2 tbsp butter, melted

pinch each of ground cumin, ground
    coriander and grated nutmeg

salt and pepper

oil for deep-frying

parsley sprigs to garnish

salad to serve

STUFFING

175 g/6 oz fresh lamb mince

1 small onion, chopped

1 tbsp pine nuts

25 g/1 oz dried apricots, chopped

pinch of grated nutmeg

pinch of ground cinnamon

1 tbsp chopped fresh coriander

2 tbsp lamb stock

1 Put the bulgur wheat in a bowl and cover with boiling water. Soak for 30 minutes, until the water has been absorbed and the bulgur wheat has swollen.

2 Meanwhile, cook the diced potatoes in a saucepan of boiling water for 10 minutes, or until cooked through. Drain and mash until smooth.

3 Add the bulgur wheat to the mashed potatoes with the beaten eggs, melted butter, ground cumin, ground coriander and nutmeg. Mix thoroughly and season to taste with salt and pepper.

4 To make the stuffing, dry-fry the lamb in a heavy-based pan for 5 minutes. Add the onion and cook for a further 2–3 minutes, then add the remaining stuffing ingredients and cook for 5 minutes, until the lamb stock has been absorbed. Leave the mixture to cool slightly, then divide into 8 portions. Roll each into a ball.

5 Divide the potato mixture into 8 portions and flatten each into a round. Place a portion of stuffing in the centre of each round. Shape the coating around the stuffing to encase it completely.

6 In a large saucepan or deep-fryer, heat the oil to180°C–190°C/ 350°F–375°F or until a cube of bread browns in 30 seconds, and cook the kibbeh, in batches if necessary, for 5–7 minutes, until golden brown. Drain, garnish and serve with salad.

potato & spinach triangles

serves four

2 tbsp butter, melted, plus extra
    for greasing
225 g/8 oz waxy potatoes,
    finely diced
500 g/1 lb 2 oz baby spinach
1 tomato, deseeded and chopped
¼ tsp chilli powder
½ tsp lemon juice
225 g/8 oz (8 sheets) filo pastry,
    thawed if frozen
salt and pepper
crisp salad, to serve
LEMON MAYONNAISE
150 ml/5 fl oz mayonnaise
2 tsp lemon juice
grated rind of 1 lemon

COOK'S TIP

Buy unwaxed or organic lemons
for grating.

---

1 Lightly grease a baking tray with a little butter.

2 Cook the potatoes in a saucepan of lightly salted, boiling water for 10 minutes, or until cooked through. Drain thoroughly and place in a large mixing bowl.

3 Meanwhile, put the spinach in a saucepan with 2 tablespoons of water, cover and cook over a low heat for 2 minutes, until wilted. Drain the spinach thoroughly, squeezing out excess moisture with the back of a spoon, and add to the potatoes.

4 Stir in the tomato, chilli powder and lemon juice. Season to taste with salt and pepper.

5 Lightly brush 8 sheets of filo pastry with melted butter. Spread out four of the sheets and lay the other four on top of each. Cut them into rectangles about 20 x 10-cm/ 8 x 4-inches.

6 Spoon a little of the potato and spinach mixture on to one end of a filo rectangle. Fold a corner of the pastry over the filling, fold the pointed end back over the pastry strip, then fold over the remaining pastry to form a triangle. Repeat with the remaining filo rectangles and filling.

7 Place the triangles on the baking tray and bake in a preheated oven, 190°C/375°F/Gas Mark , for 20 minutes, or until golden brown.

8 To make the mayonnaise, mix the mayonnaise, lemon juice and lemon rind together in a small bowl. Serve the potato and spinach filo triangles warm or cold with the lemon mayonnaise and a crisp salad.

curry pasties

serves four

225 g/8 oz plain wholemeal flour

100 g/3½ oz margarine, cut into
    small pieces

4 tbsp water

2 tbsp vegetable oil

225 g/8 oz diced root vegetables,
    such as potatoes, carrots
    and parsnips

1 small onion, chopped

2 garlic cloves, chopped finely

½ tsp curry powder

½ tsp ground turmeric

½ tsp ground cumin

½ tsp wholegrain mustard

5 tbsp vegetable stock

soya milk, to glaze

1 Place the flour in a mixing bowl
and rub in the margarine with
your fingertips until the mixture
resembles breadcrumbs. Stir in the
water and bring together to form a soft
dough. Wrap and leave to chill in the
refrigerator for 30 minutes.

2 To make the filling, heat the oil in
a large saucepan. Add the diced
root vegetables, chopped onion and

garlic and fry, stirring occasionally,
for 2 minutes. Stir in all of the spices
and the mustard, turning the
vegetables to coat. Fry the vegetables,
stirring constantly, for a further minute.

3 Add the stock to the pan and
bring to the boil. Cover and
simmer, stirring occasionally, for about
20 minutes, until the vegetables are
tender and the liquid has been
absorbed. Leave to cool.

4 Divide the pastry into four
portions. Roll each portion into a
15-cm/6-inch round. Place the filling
on one half of each round.

5 Brush the edges of each round
with soya milk, then fold over and
press the edges together to seal. Place
on a baking tray. Bake in a preheated
oven, 200°C/ 400°F/Gas Mark 6, for
25–30 minutes, until golden brown.

vegetable samosas

makes twelve

FILLING

2 tbsp vegetable oil

1 onion, chopped

½ tsp ground coriander

½ tsp ground cumin

pinch of ground turmeric

½ tsp ground ginger

½ tsp garam masala

1 garlic clove, crushed

225 g/8 oz potatoes, diced

100 g/3½ oz frozen peas, thawed

150 g/5½ oz spinach, chopped

lemon wedges to garnish

PASTRY

350 g/12 oz (12 sheets) filo pastry

oil, for deep-frying

1 To make the filling, heat the oil in a frying pan. Add the onion and sauté, stirring frequently, for 1–2 minutes, until softened. Stir in all of the spices and garlic and cook for 1 minute.

2 Add the potatoes and cook over a low heat, stirring frequently, for 5 minutes, until they begin to soften.

3 Stir in the peas and spinach and cook for a further 3–4 minutes.

4 Lay the filo pastry sheets out on a clean work surface and fold each sheet in half lengthways.

5 Place 2 tablespoons of the vegetable filling at one end of each folded pastry sheet. Fold over one corner to make a triangle. Continue folding in this way to make a triangular package and seal the edges with water.

6 Repeat with the remaining pastry and the remaining filling.

7 Heat the oil for deep-frying to 180–190°C/350–375°F or until a cube of bread browns in 30 seconds. Fry the samosas, in batches, for 1–2 minutes, until golden. Drain on absorbent kitchen paper and keep warm while cooking the remainder. Garnish and serve immediately.

creamy stuffed mushrooms

serves four

25 g/1 oz dried ceps

225 g/8 oz floury potatoes, diced

2 tbsp butter, melted

4 tbsp double cream

2 tbsp snipped fresh chives

8 large open-capped mushrooms

25 g/1 oz Emmenthal
    cheese, grated

150 ml/5 fl oz vegetable stock

salt and pepper

fresh chives, to garnish

VARIATION

Use fresh mushrooms instead of the dried ceps, if preferred, and stir a mixture of chopped nuts into the mushroom stuffing mixture for extra crunch.

1 Place the dried ceps in a small bowl. Add sufficient boiling water to cover and leave to soak for 20 minutes.

2 Meanwhile, cook the potatoes in a medium saucepan of lightly salted, boiling water for 10 minutes, until cooked through and tender. Drain well and mash until smooth.

3 Drain the soaked ceps and then chop them finely. Mix them into the mashed potato.

4 Thoroughly blend the butter, cream and snipped chives together and pour the mixture into the ceps and potato mixture, mixing well. Season to taste with salt and pepper.

5 Remove the stalks from the open-capped mushrooms. Chop the stalks and stir them into the potato mixture. Spoon the mixture into the open-capped mushrooms and sprinkle the cheese over the top.

6 Arrange the filled mushrooms in a shallow ovenproof dish and pour in the vegetable stock.

7 Cover the dish and cook in a preheated oven, 220°C/425°F/ Gas Mark 7, for 20 minutes. Remove the lid and cook for a further 5 minutes, until golden. Serve the mushrooms immediately, garnished with chives.

vegetable-stuffed parathas

serves six

DOUGH

225 g/8 oz wholemeal flour (ata
or chapati flour), plus extra
for dusting

½ tsp salt

200 ml/7 fl oz water

about 4 tbsp vegetable ghee

FILLING

675 g/1½ lb potatoes

½ tsp ground turmeric

1 tsp garam masala

1 tsp finely chopped fresh
root ginger

1 tbsp chopped fresh coriander
leaves

3 fresh green chillies, deseeded and
chopped finely

1 tsp salt

1 For the paratas, mix the flour, salt,
water and 1¼ teaspoons of the
ghee in a bowl to form a dough.

2 Divide the dough into 6 equal
portions. Roll each portion out
on a floured work surface. Brush
the middle of each of the dough
portions with ½ teaspoon of the
remaining ghee. Fold the dough
portions in half, roll into a pipe-like
shape, flatten with the palms of your
hands, then roll around a finger to
form a coil. Roll out again, using flour
to dust when necessary, to form a round
about 18-cm/7-inches in diameter.

3 To make the filling, place the
potatoes in a large saucepan of
boiling water and cook until soft
enough to be mashed.

4 Blend the turmeric, garam
masala, ginger, coriander leaves,
chillies and salt together in a bowl.

5 Add the spice mixture to the
mashed potato and mix well.
Spread about 1 tablespoon of the spicy
potato mixture on each dough portion
and cover with another rolled-out piece
of dough. Seal the edges well.

6 Heat 2 teaspoons of the
remaining ghee in a heavy-based
frying pan. Place the parathas gently in
the pan, in batches, and fry, turning
and moving them about gently with a
flat spoon, until golden. Add more
ghee as required.

7 Remove the parathas from the
frying pan and serve immediately.

COOK'S TIP

Clarified butter, known as ghee,
was once the main cooking fat in
India and Pakistan. It has largely
been superseded by vegetable
ghee, usually corn oil.

smoked fish & potato pâté

serves four

650 g/1 lb 7 oz floury
    potatoes, diced

300 g/10½ oz smoked mackerel
    fillets, skinned and flaked

75 g/2¾ oz cooked gooseberries

2 tsp lemon juice

2 tbsp low-fat crème fraîche

1 tbsp capers

1 gherkin, chopped

1 tbsp chopped dill pickle

1 tbsp chopped fresh dill

salt and pepper

lemon wedges, to garnish

toast or warm crusty bread, to serve

1 Cook the diced potatoes in a large saucepan of boiling water for 10 minutes, until tender, then drain well.

2 Place the cooked potatoes in a food processor or blender.

3 Add the skinned and flaked smoked mackerel and process for 30 seconds, until fairly smooth. Alternatively, place the ingredients in a bowl and then mash them with a fork.

4 Add the cooked gooseberries, lemon juice and crème fraîche to the fish and potato mixture. Blend for a further 10 seconds or mash well.

5 Stir in the capers, gherkin, dill pickle, and fresh dill. Season well with salt and pepper.

6 Turn the fish pâté into a serving dish, garnish with lemon wedges and serve with slices of toast or warm crusty bread cut into chunks or slices.

COOK'S TIP

Use stewed, canned or bottled cooked gooseberries for convenience and to save time, or when fresh gooseberries are out of season.

potato & pepperoni pizza

serves four

1 tbsp butter, plus extra for greasing

plain flour, for dusting

900 g/2 lb floury potatoes, diced

1 tbsp butter

2 garlic cloves, crushed

2 tbsp chopped mixed fresh herbs

1 egg, beaten

6 tbsp passata

2 tbsp tomato purée

50 g/1¾ oz pepperoni slices

1 green pepper, deseeded and
    cut into strips

1 yellow pepper, deseeded and
    cut into strips

2 large open-cap mushrooms, sliced

25 g/1 oz stoned black olives,
    quartered

125 g/4½ oz mozzarella
    cheese, sliced

preheated oven, 220°C/425°F/Gas
Mark 7, for 7–10 minutes, until set.

3 Mix the passata and tomato
purée together and spoon it over
the pizza base, to within 1-cm/½-inch
of the edge of the base.

4 Arrange the pepperoni slices and
the peppers, mushrooms and
olives on top of the passata.

1 Grease and flour a 23-cm/9-inch
pizza pan. Cook the potatoes in a
pan of boiling water for 10 minutes, or
until tender. Drain and mash, then
transfer to a mixing bowl and stir in the
butter, garlic, herbs and egg.

2 Spread the mixture into the
prepared pizza pan. Cook in a

5 Scatter the mozzarella cheese
on top of the pizza. Return to the
oven for 20 minutes, or until the base
is cooked through and the cheese has
melted on top. Serve hot.

potato & tomato calzone

serves four

DOUGH

450 g/1 lb strong white bread flour,
    plus extra for dusting

1 tsp easy-blend dried yeast

300 ml/10 fl oz vegetable stock

1 tbsp clear honey

1 tsp caraway seeds

vegetable oil, for greasing

skimmed milk, for glazing

FILLING

1 tbsp vegetable oil

225 g/8 oz waxy potatoes, diced

1 onion, halved and sliced

2 garlic cloves, crushed

40 g/1½ oz sun-dried tomatoes

2 tbsp chopped fresh basil

2 tbsp tomato purée

2 celery sticks, sliced

50 g/1¾ oz mozzarella
    cheese, grated

COOK'S TIP

Mozzarella di buffala, made from
the milk of the water buffalo,
has the best flavour.

---

1 To make the dough, sift the flour into a large mixing bowl and stir in the yeast. Make a well in the centre of the mixture. Stir in the stock, honey and caraway seeds and bring the mixture together to form a dough.

2 Turn the dough out on to a lightly floured surface and knead for 8 minutes, until smooth. Place the dough in a lightly oiled mixing bowl, cover with lightly oiled clingfilm and leave to rise in a warm place for 1 hour, or until it has doubled in size.

3 Meanwhile, make the filling. Heat the oil in a frying pan and add all the remaining ingredients except for the cheese. Cook for about 5 minutes, stirring.

4 Divide the risen dough into 4 pieces. On a lightly floured surface, roll them out to form 4 x 18-cm/ 7-inch rounds. Spoon equal amounts of the filling on to one half of each round. Sprinkle the cheese over the filling. Brush the edge of the dough with milk and fold the dough over to form 4 semi-circles, pressing to seal the edges.

5 Place on a non-stick baking tray and brush with milk. Cook in a preheated oven, 220°C/425°F/Gas Mark 7, for 30 minutes, until golden and risen. Serve immediately.

salt cod hash

serves four

25 g/1 oz sea salt

750 g/1 lb 10 oz cod fillet

4 eggs

3 tbsp olive oil, plus extra
    for drizzling

8 rindless smoked streaky bacon
    rashers, chopped

700 g/1 lb 9 oz old potatoes, diced

8 garlic cloves

8 thick slices good-quality
    white bread

2 plum tomatoes, skinned
    and chopped

2 tsp red wine vinegar

2 tbsp chopped fresh parsley, plus
    extra to garnish

salt and pepper

lemon wedges,
    to garnish

1 Sprinkle the sea salt over both sides of the cod fillet. Place in a shallow dish, cover with clingfilm and chill for 48 hours. When ready to cook, remove the cod from the refrigerator and rinse thoroughly under cold water. Place in a shallow dish, cover with cold water and leave to soak for 2 hours, then drain well.

2 Bring a large saucepan of water to the boil and add the fish. Remove the pan from the heat and leave for 10 minutes.

3 Drain the fish on kitchen paper and flake the flesh. Reserve. Discard the soaking water.

4 Bring a saucepan of water to the boil. Add the eggs, bring back to the boil, and simmer for 7–9 minutes from when the water returns to the boil: 7 minutes for a slightly soft centre, 9 for a firm centre. Drain, then plunge the eggs into cold water. Shell the eggs and roughly chop. Reserve.

5 Heat the oil in a large frying pan and add the bacon. Cook over a medium heat for 4–5 minutes, until crisp. Remove and drain on kitchen paper. Put the potatoes and garlic in the pan and cook over a medium heat for 8–10 minutes, until crisp and golden. Meanwhile, toast the bread on both sides. Drizzle the bread with olive oil and reserve.

6 Add the tomatoes, bacon, fish, vinegar and egg to the potatoes and garlic. Cook for 2 minutes. Stir in the parsley and season. Put the toast on to serving plates, top with the hash and garnish with parsley and lemon.

pepper & mushroom hash

serves four

675 g/1lb 8 oz potatoes, diced

1 tbsp olive oil

2 garlic cloves, crushed

1 green pepper, deseeded
   and diced

1 yellow pepper, deseeded
   and diced

3 tomatoes, diced

75 g/2¾ oz button
   mushrooms, halved

1 tbsp Worcestershire sauce

2 tbsp chopped fresh basil

salt and pepper

fresh basil leaves, to garnish

warm crusty bread, to serve

COOK'S TIP

Most brands of Worcestershire
sauce contain anchovies, so if
you are a vegetarian, check the
label to make sure you choose
a vegetarian variety.

1 Cook the diced potatoes in a
large saucepan of lightly salted,
boiling water for 7–8 minutes. Drain
well and reserve.

2 Heat the olive oil in a large,
heavy-based frying pan. Add the
potatoes and cook over a medium
heat, stirring constantly, for about
8–10 minutes, until browned.

3 Add the garlic and peppers and
cook, stirring frequently, for
2–3 minutes.

4 Stir in the tomatoes and
mushrooms and cook, stirring
frequently, for 5–6 minutes.

5 Stir in the Worcestershire sauce
and basil and season to taste with
salt and pepper. Transfer to a warm
serving dish, garnish with basil sprigs
and serve with warm crusty bread.

hash browns & tomato sauce

serves four

500 g/1 lb 2 oz waxy potatoes

1 carrot, diced

1 celery stick, diced

55 g/2 oz button mushrooms, diced

1 onion, diced

2 garlic cloves, crushed

25 g/1 oz frozen peas, thawed

55 g/2 oz Parmesan cheese,
  freshly grated

4 tbsp vegetable oil

2 tbsp butter

salt and pepper

SAUCE

300 ml/10 fl oz passata

2 tbsp chopped fresh coriander

1 tbsp Worcestershire sauce

½ tsp chilli powder

2 tsp brown sugar

2 tsp American mustard

5 tbsp vegetable stock

1 Cook the potatoes in a saucepan of lightly salted, boiling water for 10 minutes. Drain and leave to cool. Meanwhile, cook the carrot in lightly salted, boiling water for 5 minutes.

2 When the potatoes are cool enough to handle, grate them with a coarse grater.

3 Drain the carrot and add it to the grated potatoes, together with the celery, mushrooms, onion, garlic, peas and cheese. Season to taste with salt and pepper.

4 Put all of the sauce ingredients in a small saucepan and bring to the boil. Reduce the heat to low and simmer for 15 minutes.

5 Divide the potato mixture into 8 portions of equal size and shape into flattened rectangles with your hands.

6 Heat the oil and butter in a frying pan and cook the hash browns, in batches, over a low heat for 4–5 minutes on each side, until crisp and golden brown.

7 Transfer the hash browns to a serving plate and serve immediately with the tomato sauce.

VARIATION

For an extra spicy tomato sauce, add 1 deseeded and chopped finely fresh green chilli with the other ingredients in step 4.

potato & cauliflower fritters

serves four

225 g/8 oz floury potatoes, diced

225 g/8 oz cauliflower florets

35 g/1¼ oz Parmesan cheese,
    freshly grated

1 egg

1 egg white, for coating

oil, for frying

paprika, for dusting (optional)

salt and pepper

crispy bacon slices, chopped,
    to serve

1 Cook the potatoes in a saucepan of boiling water for 10 minutes, until cooked through. Drain well and mash until smooth.

2 Meanwhile, cook the cauliflower florets in a separate pan of boiling water for 10 minutes.

3 Drain the cauliflower florets and then add them to the mashed potato. Gently stir in the grated Parmesan cheese and season to taste with salt and pepper.

4 Separate the whole egg and beat the yolk into the potato and cauliflower, mixing well.

5 Lightly whisk both the egg whites in a clean bowl, then carefully fold into the potato and cauliflower mixture.

6 Divide the potato mixture into 8 equal portions and then shape them into rounds.

7 Heat the oil in a frying pan and cook the fritters for 3–5 minutes, turning once halfway through cooking. Dust the cooked fritters with a little paprika, if desired, and then serve them at once accompanied by the crispy chopped bacon.

fritters with garlic sauce

serves four

500 g/1 lb 2 oz waxy
    potatoes, diced
125 g/4½ oz Parmesan cheese,
    freshly grated
vegetable oil, for deep-frying
SAUCE
2 tbsp butter
1 onion, halved and sliced
2 garlic cloves, crushed
2½ tbsp plain flour
300 ml/10 fl oz milk
1 tbsp chopped fresh parsley
BATTER
5 tbsp plain flour
1 small egg
150 ml/5 fl oz milk

1 To make the sauce, melt the butter in a saucepan and cook the onion and garlic over a low heat, stirring frequently, for 2–3 minutes. Add the flour and cook, stirring constantly, for 1 minute.

2 Remove the pan from the heat and stir in the milk and parsley. Return the pan to the heat and bring to the boil, stirring constantly. Remove and keep warm.

3 Meanwhile, cook the diced potatoes in a saucepan of boiling water for 5–10 minutes, until just firm. Do not overcook or they will fall apart.

4 Drain the potatoes and toss them in the Parmesan cheese. If the potatoes are still slightly wet, the cheese will stick to them and coat them well.

5 To make the batter, place the flour in a mixing bowl and gradually beat in the egg and milk until smooth. Dip the potato cubes into the batter to coat them.

6 In a large saucepan or deep-fat fryer, heat the oil to 180–190°C/350–375°F or until a cube of bread

browns in 30 seconds. Add the fritters and cook for 3–4 minutes, or until golden. brown all over

7 Remove the fritters with a slotted spoon and drain well. Transfer them to a warm serving bowl and serve with the garlic sauce.

85

croquettes with ham

serves four

450 g/1 lb floury potatoes, diced

300 ml/10 fl oz milk

2 tbsp butter

4 spring onions, chopped

75 g/2¾ oz Cheddar cheese, grated

50 g/1¾ oz smoked ham, chopped

1 celery stick, diced

1 egg, beaten

5 tbsp plain flour

vegetable oil, for deep-frying

salt and pepper

COATING

2 eggs, beaten

125 g/4½ oz fresh

· wholemeal breadcrumbs

SAUCE

2 tbsp butter

2 tbsp plain flour

150 ml/5 fl oz milk

150 ml/5 fl oz vegetable stock

75 g/2¾ oz Cheddar cheese, grated

1 tsp Dijon mustard

1 tbsp chopped fresh coriander

TO GARNISH

tomato and cucumber wedges

1 Place the potatoes in a pan with the milk and bring to the boil. Reduce to a simmer until the liquid has been absorbed and the potatoes are cooked.

2 Add the butter and mash the potatoes. Stir in the spring onions, cheese, ham, celery, egg and flour. Season and leave to cool.

3 To make the coating, whisk the eggs in a bowl. Put the breadcrumbs in a separate bowl.

4 Shape the potato mixture into 8 balls. First dip them in the egg, then in the breadcrumbs.

5 To make the sauce, melt the butter in a small pan. Add the flour and cook for 1 minute. Remove from the heat and stir in the milk, stock, cheese, mustard and coriander. Bring to the boil, stirring until thickened. Reduce the heat and keep warm, stirring occasionally.

6 In a deep-fat fryer, heat the oil to 180–190°C/350–375°F or until a cube of bread browns in 30 seconds. Fry the croquettes in batches for 5 minutes, until golden. Drain well, garnish and serve with the sauce.

VARIATION
Substitute cooked smoked chicken for the ham and Fontina cheese for the Cheddar.

pakoras

serves four

6 tbsp gram flour

½ tsp salt

1 tsp chilli powder

1 tsp baking powder

1½ tsp white cumin seeds

1 tsp pomegranate seeds

300 ml/10 fl oz water

1 tbsp chopped fresh coriander plus
    sprigs for garnush

vegetables of your choice:
    cauliflower cut into small florets,
    onions, cut into rings, sliced
    potatoes, sliced aubergines or
    peppers, deseeded and cut into
    strips

vegetable oil, for deep-frying

1 Sift the gram flour into a large mixing bowl. Add the salt, chilli powder, baking powder, cumin and pomegranate seeds and blend together well. Pour in the water and beat thoroughly to form a smooth batter.

2 Add the coriander and mix well. Reserve the batter until required.

3 Heat the oil in a deep-fat fryer to 180°C. Dip the prepared vegetables into the batter, a few at a time, carefully shaking off any excess.

COOK'S TIP

When deep-frying, it is important to use oil at the correct temperature. If the oil is too hot, the outside of the food will burn, as will the spices, before the inside is cooked. If the oil is too cool, the food will be sodden with oil before the batter becomes crisp.

4 When the oil has reached the correct temperature, carefully add the battered vegetables and deep-fry, in batches, turning once.

5 Repeat this process until all of the batter has been used up.

6 Transfer the cooked vegetables to kitchen paper and drain thoroughly. Garnish and serve.

chicken & herb fritters

serves four

500 g/1 lb 2 oz mashed potato, with butter added

225 g/8 oz chopped, cooked, skinless, boneless chicken

115 g/4 oz cooked ham, chopped finely

1 tbsp mixed fresh herbs

2 eggs, lightly beaten

milk

fresh brown breadcrumbs

vegetable oil, for frying

salt and pepper

fresh parsley sprig, to garnish

salad leaves, to serve

1 In a large bowl, blend the potatoes, chicken, ham, herbs and 1 egg, and season well.

2 Shape the mixture into small balls or flat pancakes.

3 Add a little milk to the second egg and mix together.

COOK'S TIP

A mixture of chopped fresh tarragon and parsley makes a fresh and flavoursome addition to these tasty fritters.

4 Place the breadcrumbs on a plate. Dip the balls in the egg and milk mixture, then roll in the breadcrumbs to coat them completely.

5 Heat the vegetable oil in a large frying pan and fry the fritters until they are golden brown. Garnish with a sprig of fresh parsley and serve at once with fresh salad leaves.

vegetable kebabs

makes twelve

600 g/1 lb 5 oz potatoes, sliced

1 medium onion, sliced

½ medium cauliflower, cut into
   small florets

50 g/1¾ oz cooked peas

1 tbsp spinach purée

2–3 fresh green chillies

1 tbsp fresh coriander leaves

1 tsp finely chopped fresh
   root ginger

1 tsp crushed garlic

1 tsp ground coriander

pinch of ground turmeric

1 tsp salt

50 g/1¾ oz breadcrumbs

300 ml/10 fl oz vegetable oil

fresh chilli strips, to garnish

1 Place the potatoes, onion and cauliflower florets in a large pan of water and bring to the boil. Reduce the heat and simmer gently until the potatoes are cooked through and tender. Remove the vegetables from the pan with a slotted spoon and drain thoroughly. Reserve.

2 Add the peas and spinach to the vegetables and mix, mashing down thoroughly with a fork.

3 Using a sharp knife, finely chop the green chillies and the fresh coriander leaves.

4 Mix the green chillies and fresh coriander leaves with the ginger, garlic, ground coriander, ground turmeric and salt.

5 Blend the spice mixture into the vegetables, mixing with a fork to make a paste.

6 Scatter the breadcrumbs on to a large plate.

7 Break off 10–12 small balls from the spice paste. Flatten them with the palm of your hand or with a palette knife to make flat, round shapes.

8 Dip each kebab in the breadcrumbs, coating well.

9 Heat the oil in a heavy-based frying-pan and fry the kebabs, in batches, until golden brown, turning occasionally. Transfer to serving plates and garnish with fresh chilli strips. Serve hot.

cheese & onion röstis

serves four

900 g/2 lb potatoes

1 onion, grated

50 g/1¾ oz Gruyère cheese, grated

2 tbsp chopped fresh parsley

1 tbsp olive oil

2 tbsp butter

salt and pepper

TO GARNISH

1 spring onion, shredded

1 small tomato, quartered

1 Parboil the potatoes in a pan of lightly salted, boiling water for 10 minutes and leave to cool. Peel the potatoes and grate with a coarse grater. Place the grated potatoes in a large mixing bowl.

2 Stir in the onion, cheese and parsley. Season well with salt and pepper. Divide the potato mixture into 4 portions of equal size and form them into cakes.

3 Heat half of the olive oil with half the butter in a frying pan and cook 2 of the potato cakes over a high heat for 1 minute, then reduce the heat and cook for 5 minutes, until they are golden underneath. Turn them over and cook for a further 5 minutes.

4 Repeat with the other half of the olive oil and the remaining butter to cook the remaining 2 potato cakes. Transfer the röstis to warm individual serving plates, garnish with shredded spring onion and tomato quarters and serve immediately.

COOK'S TIP

The potato cakes should be flattened as much as possible during cooking, otherwise the outsides will be cooked before the centres are done.

sweet potato cakes

serves four

500 g/1 lb 2 oz sweet potatoes

2 garlic cloves, crushed

1 small fresh green chilli, deseeded
and chopped

2 fresh coriander sprigs, chopped

1 tbsp dark soy sauce

plain flour, for shaping

vegetable oil, for frying

sesame seeds, for sprinkling

SOY-TOMATO SAUCE

2 tsp vegetable oil

1 garlic clove, chopped finely

1½ tsp finely chopped fresh
root ginger

3 tomatoes, skinned and chopped

2 tbsp dark soy sauce

1 tbsp lime juice

2 tbsp chopped fresh coriander

1 To make the soy-tomato sauce, heat the oil in a wok and stir-fry the garlic and ginger over a medium heat for about 1 minute. Add the tomatoes and stir-fry for a further 2 minutes. Remove the wok from the heat and stir in the soy sauce, lime juice and chopped coriander. Reserve and keep warm.

2 Peel the sweet potatoes and grate finely (you can do this quickly with a food processor). Place the garlic, chilli and coriander in a mortar and crush to a smooth paste with a pestle. Stir in the soy sauce and mix with the sweet potatoes.

3 Divide the mixture into 12 equal portions. Dip into flour and pat into a flat, round patty shape.

4 Heat a shallow layer of oil in a wide frying pan. Fry the sweet potato patties, in batches, over a high heat until golden, turning once.

5 Drain the sweet potato cakes on kitchen paper and sprinkle with sesame seeds. Transfer to a warm serving dish and serve hot, with the soy-tomato sauce.

potato & spinach gnocchi

serves four

300 g/10½ oz floury potatoes, diced

175 g/6 oz spinach

1 egg yolk

1 tsp olive oil

125 g/4½ oz plain flour

salt and pepper

spinach leaves, to garnish

SAUCE

1 tbsp olive oil

2 shallots, chopped

1 garlic clove, crushed

300 ml/10 fl oz passata

2 tsp soft light brown sugar

VARIATION

Add chopped fresh herbs
and cheese to the gnocchi
dough instead of the
spinach, if you prefer.

1 Cook the diced potatoes in a saucepan of boiling water for 10 minutes, or until cooked through. Drain thoroughly, then mash.

2 Meanwhile, in a separate pan, blanch the spinach in a little boiling water for 1–2 minutes. Drain the spinach and shred the leaves.

3 Transfer the mashed potato to a lightly floured chopping board and make a well in the centre. Add the egg yolk, olive oil, spinach, salt and pepper and a little of the flour and quickly mix the ingredients into the potato, adding more flour as you go, until you have a firm dough. Divide the mixture into very small dumplings.

4 Cook the gnocchi, in batches, in a saucepan of lightly salted, boiling water for about 5 minutes, or until they rise to the surface.

5 Meanwhile, to make the sauce, put the olive oil, shallots, garlic, passata and sugar into a saucepan and cook over a low heat, stirring frequently for 10–15 minutes, or until the sauce has thickened.

6 Drain the gnocchi using a slotted spoon and transfer to warm serving dishes. Spoon the sauce over the gnocchi and garnish with the fresh spinach leaves.

vegetable cake

serves four

BASE

2 tbsp vegetable oil, plus extra
   for brushing

1.25 kg/2 lb 12 oz waxy potatoes,
   sliced thinly

TOPPING

1 tbsp vegetable oil

1 leek, chopped

1 courgette, grated

1 red pepper, deseeded and diced

1 green pepper, deseeded and diced

1 carrot, grated

2 tsp chopped fresh parsley

225 g/8 oz full-fat soft cheese

25 g/1 oz mature cheese, grated

2 eggs, beaten

salt and pepper

shredded cooked leek, to garnish

salad, to serve

1 Brush a 20-cm/8-inch springform
cake tin with oil.

2 To make the base, heat the oil
in a frying pan. Cook the potato
slices until softened and browned.
Drain on kitchen paper and place in
the base of the tin.

3 To make the topping, heat the
vegetable oil in a separate frying
pan. Add the chopped leek and fry
over a low heat, stirring frequently, for
3–4 minutes, until softened.

4 Add the courgette, red and green
peppers, carrot and chopped
parsley to the pan and cook over a
low heat for 5–7 minutes, or until the
vegetables have softened.

5 Meanwhile, beat the soft and
mature cheeses and eggs
together in a bowl. Stir in the cooked
vegetables and season to taste with
salt and pepper. Spoon the mixture
evenly over the potato slices in the
base of the tin.

6 Cook in a preheated oven,
190°C/ 375°F/Gas Mark 5, for
20–25 minutes, until the cake is set.

7 Remove the vegetable cake from
the tin, transfer to a warm serving
plate, garnish with shredded leek and
serve with a crisp salad.

feta & spinach omelette

serves four

75 g/2¾ oz butter

1.3 kg/3 lb waxy potatoes, diced

3 garlic cloves, crushed

1 tsp paprika

2 tomatoes, skinned, deseeded
and diced

12 eggs

pepper

FILLING

225 g/8 oz baby spinach

1 tsp fennel seeds

125 g/4½ oz feta cheese, diced
(drained weight)

4 tbsp natural yogurt

1 Heat 2 tablespoons of the butter in a frying pan and cook the potatoes over a low heat, stirring constantly, for 7–10 minutes, until golden. Transfer to a bowl.

2 Add the garlic, paprika and tomatoes to the pan and cook for a further 2 minutes.

3 Whisk the eggs together and season with pepper. Pour the eggs into the potatoes and mix well.

4 For the filling, cook the spinach in boiling water for 1 minute, until just wilted. Drain and refresh under cold running water. Pat dry with kitchen paper. Stir in the fennel seeds, feta cheese and yogurt.

5 Heat a quarter of the remaining butter in a 15-cm/6-inch omelette pan. Ladle a quarter of the egg and potato mixture into the pan. Cook, turning once, for 2 minutes, until set.

6 Transfer the omelette to a warm serving plate. Spoon a quarter of the spinach mixture on to one half of the omelette, then fold the omelette in half over the filling. Repeat to make a further 3 omelettes.

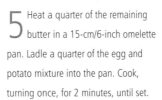

97

baked potatoes with salsa

serves four

4 baking potatoes

1 large ripe avocado

1 tsp lemon juice

175 g/6 oz smoked tofu, diced

2 garlic cloves, crushed

1 onion, chopped finely

1 tomato, chopped finely

125 g/4½ oz mixed salad leaves

fresh coriander sprigs, to garnish

SALSA

2 ripe tomatoes, deseeded
    and diced

1 tbsp chopped fresh coriander

1 shallot, diced finely

1 fresh green chilli, deseeded
    and diced

1 tbsp lemon juice

salt and pepper

1 Scrub the potatoes and prick the skins with a fork. Rub a little salt into the skins and place them on a baking tray.

2 Cook in a preheated oven, 190°C/ 375°F/Gas Mark 5, for 1 hour, or until cooked through and the skins are crisp.

3 Cut the potatoes in half lengthways and scoop the flesh into a bowl, leaving a thin layer of potato inside the shells.

4 Halve and stone the avocado. Using a teaspoon, scoop out the avocado flesh and add it to the bowl containing the potato. Stir in the lemon juice and mash the mixture together with a fork until fairly smooth. Mix in the tofu, garlic, onion and tomato. Spoon the mixture into one half of the potato shells.

5 Arrange the salad leaves over the avocado mixture and place the other half of the potato shell on top.

6 To make the salsa, mix the tomatoes, coriander, shallot, chilli, lemon juice and salt and pepper to taste in a bowl. Garnish the potatoes with sprigs of fresh coriander and serve with the salsa.

COOK'S TIP

Avocados vary in colour from brownish purple to green, the skin may be smooth or knobbly and the shape varies from small and relatively round to long and pear-shaped. Whatever variety you buy, test for ripeness by gently cupping the stalk end. It should just yield to pressure, but should not be soft or squashy. Use ripe avocados immediately.

pesto jackets

serves four

4 baking potatoes

150 ml/5 fl oz double cream

5 tbsp vegetable stock

1 tbsp lemon juice

2 garlic cloves, crushed

3 tbsp chopped fresh basil

2 tbsp pine kernels

35 g/1¼ oz Parmesan cheese,
   freshly grated

salt and pepper

1 Scrub the potatoes well and prick the skins with a fork. Rub a little salt into the skins and place on a baking tray.

2 Cook in a preheated oven, 190°C/ 375°F/Gas Mark 5, for 1 hour, or until the potatoes are cooked through and the skins are crisp.

3 Remove the potatoes from the oven and cut them in half lengthways. Using a spoon, scoop the potato flesh into a mixing bowl, leaving a thin shell of potato inside the skins. Mash the potato flesh with a fork.

4 Meanwhile, mix the cream and vegetable stock in a saucepan and simmer over a low heat for about 8–10 minutes, or until reduced by half.

5 Stir in the lemon juice, garlic and chopped basil and season to taste with salt and pepper. Stir the mixture into the mashed potato flesh, together with the pine kernels.

6 Spoon the mixture back into the potato shells and sprinkle the Parmesan cheese on top. Return the potatoes to the oven for 10 minutes, or until the cheese has browned. Serve hot.

jacket potatoes with beans

serves six

1.8 kg/4 lb potatoes

4 tbsp vegetable ghee or oil

1 large onion, chopped

2 garlic cloves, crushed

1 tsp ground turmeric

1 tbsp cumin seeds

2 tbsp mild or medium curry paste

350 g/12 oz cherry tomatoes, halved

400 g/14 oz canned black-eyed beans, drained and rinsed

400 g/14 oz canned red kidney beans, drained and rinsed

1 tbsp lemon juice

2 tbsp tomato purée

150 ml/5 fl oz water

2 tbsp chopped fresh mint or coriander

salt and pepper

1 Scrub the potatoes and prick several times with a fork. Place in a preheated oven, 180°C/350°F/Gas Mark 4, and cook for 1–1¼ hours, or until the potatoes are cooked through.

2 About 20 minutes before the end of cooking time, prepare the topping. Heat the ghee or oil in a saucepan, add the onion and cook over a low heat, stirring frequently, for 5 minutes. Add the garlic, turmeric, cumin seeds and curry paste and cook gently for 1 minute.

3 Stir in the tomatoes, black-eyed beans and red kidney beans, lemon juice, tomato purée, water and mint or coriander. Season to taste with salt and pepper, then cover and simmer over a low heat, stirring frequently, for 10 minutes.

4 When the potatoes are cooked, cut them in half and mash the flesh lightly with a fork. Spoon the prepared bean mixture on top, place on warm, individual serving plates and serve immediately.

sweet potato & leek patties

serves four

900 g/2 lb sweet potatoes

4 tsp sunflower oil

2 leeks, trimmed and chopped finely

1 garlic clove, crushed

2 tsp finely chopped fresh
 root ginger

200 g/7 oz canned
 sweetcorn, drained

2 tbsp low-fat natural fromage frais

6 tbsp wholemeal flour

salt and pepper

GINGER SAUCE

2 tbsp white wine vinegar

2 tsp caster sugar

1 fresh red chilli, deseeded
 and chopped

2.5-cm/1-inch piece fresh root
 ginger, cut into thin strips

2 tbsp ginger wine

4 tbsp vegetable stock

1 tsp cornflour

TO SERVE

lettuce leaves

spring onions, shredded

2 Heat 2 teaspoons of the oil and fry the leeks, garlic and ginger for 2–3 minutes. Stir into the potato with the sweetcorn, seasoning and fromage frais. Form into 8 patties and toss in the flour. Chill for 30 minutes. Place the patties on a grill rack and lightly brush with the remaining oil. Grill for 5 minutes, then turn over, brush with oil and grill for a further 5 minutes.

3 To make the sauce, place the vinegar, sugar, chilli and ginger in a pan and simmer for 5 minutes. Stir in the wine. Blend the stock and cornflour and add to the sauce, stirring, until thickened. Serve the patties with lettuce and spring onions, and the sauce.

1 Peel the potatoes, dice and boil for 10–15 minutes. Drain well and mash. Leave to cool.

mixed mushroom cakes

serves four

500 g/1 lb 2 oz floury
   potatoes, diced

2 tbsp butter

175 g/6 oz mixed
   mushrooms, chopped

2 garlic cloves, crushed

1 small egg, beaten

1 tbsp snipped fresh chives,
   plus extra to garnish

plain flour, for dusting

vegetable oil, for frying

salt and pepper

salad, to serve

1 Cook the potatoes in a pan of lightly salted, boiling water for 10 minutes, or until cooked through.

2 Drain the potatoes well, mash with a potato masher or fork and reserve.

3 Meanwhile, melt the butter in a frying pan. Add the mushrooms and garlic and cook, stirring constantly, for 5 minutes. Drain well.

4 Stir the mushrooms and garlic into the potatoes, together with the beaten egg and chives.

5 Divide the mixture equally into 4 portions and shape them into round cakes with your hands. Toss them in the flour until the outsides of the cakes are completely coated, shaking off any excess.

6 Heat the oil in a frying pan. Add the potato cakes and fry over a medium heat for 10 minutes. until they are golden brown, turning them over halfway through. Serve the cakes at once, with a simple crisp salad.

prawn röstis

serves four

350 g/12 oz potatoes

350 g/12 oz celeriac

1 carrot

½ small onion

225 g/8 oz cooked peeled prawns,
   thawed if frozen and well-
   drained on kitchen paper

2½ tbsp plain flour

1 egg, lightly beaten

vegetable oil, for frying

salt and pepper

salad leaves to serve

CHERRY TOMATO SALSA

225 g/8 oz mixed cherry tomatoes
   such as baby plum, yellow or
   orange, quartered

½ small mango, finely diced

1 fresh red chilli, deseeded and
   chopped finely

½ small red onion, chopped finely

1 tbsp chopped fresh coriander

1 tbsp snipped fresh chives

2 tbsp olive oil

2 tsp lemon juice

salt and pepper

1 For the salsa, mix the tomatoes, mango, chilli, onion, coriander, chives, olive oil, lemon juice, and seasoning. Leave to allow the flavours to infuse.

2 Using a food processor or the fine blade of a box grater, finely grate the potatoes, celeriac, carrot and onion. Mix together with the prawns, flour and egg. Season well and reserve.

3 Divide the prawn mixture into eight equal pieces. Press each into a greased 10-cm/4-inch cutter (if you only have one cutter, you can simply shape the röstis individually).

4 In a large frying pan, heat a shallow layer of oil. When hot, transfer the prawn cakes, still in the cutters, to the frying pan, in four batches if necessary. When the oil sizzles underneath, remove the cutter. Fry gently, pressing down with a spatula, for 6–8 minutes on each side, until crisp and browned and the vegetables are tender. Drain on kitchen paper and keep warm in a preheated oven. Serve hot with salad and salsa.

salmon pancakes

serves four

450 g/1 lb floury potatoes, grated

2 spring onions, chopped

2 tbsp self-raising flour

2 eggs, beaten

2 tbsp vegetable oil

salt and pepper

fresh chives, to garnish

TOPPING

150 ml/5 fl oz soured cream

125 g/4½ oz smoked salmon

1 Rinse the grated potatoes under cold running water, drain and pat dry on kitchen paper. Transfer to a mixing bowl.

2 Mix the spring onions, flour and eggs into the potatoes and season well with salt and pepper.

3 Heat 1 tablespoon of the oil in a frying pan. Drop about 4 tablespoonfuls of the mixture into the pan and spread each one with the

back of a spoon to form a round (the mixture should make 16 pancakes). Cook for 5–7 minutes, turning once, until golden. Drain well.

4 Heat the remaining oil and cook the remaining mixture in batches.

5 Top the pancakes with the soured cream and smoked salmon, garnish with fresh chives and serve hot.

tuna fishcakes

serves four

225 g/8 oz potatoes, diced

1 tbsp olive oil

1 large shallot, chopped finely

1 garlic clove, chopped finely

1 tsp fresh thyme leaves

400 g/14 oz canned tuna in olive
   oil, drained

grated rind ½ lemon

1 tbsp chopped fresh parsley

2–3 tbsp plain flour

1 egg, lightly beaten

115 g/4 oz fresh breadcrumbs

vegetable oil, for shallow frying

salt and pepper

salad to serve

QUICK TOMATO SAUCE

2 tbsp olive oil

400 g/14 oz canned chopped
   tomatoes

1 garlic clove, crushed

½ tsp sugar

grated rind ½ lemon

1 tbsp chopped fresh basil

1 For the tuna fishcakes, cook the potatoes in plenty of boiling salted water for 12–15 minutes, until tender. Mash, leaving a few lumps, and reserve.

2 Heat the oil in a small frying pan and cook the shallot gently for 5 minutes, until softened. Add the garlic and thyme leaves and cook for 1 minute more. Allow to cool slightly, then add to the potatoes with the tuna, lemon rind, parsley and seasoning. Mix together well but leave some texture.

3 Form the mixture into 6–8 cakes. Dip the cakes first in the flour, then in the egg and, finally, in the breadcrumbs to coat. Chill for at least 30 minutes.

4 For the tomato sauce, put the olive oil, tomatoes, garlic, sugar, lemon rind, basil and seasoning into a saucepan and bring to the boil. Cover and simmer for 30 minutes. Uncover and simmer for 15 minutes more, until thickened.

5 Heat enough oil in a frying pan to cover the base generously. Fry the fishcakes, in batches, for 3–4 minutes each side, until golden and crisp. Drain on kitchen paper while you fry the remaining fishcakes. Serve hot with the tomato sauce and salad.

potato stir fry

serves four

900 g/2 lb waxy potatoes

2 tbsp vegetable oil

1 yellow pepper, deseeded
    and diced

1 red pepper, deseeded and diced

1 carrot, cut into matchsticks

1 courgette, cut into matchsticks

2 garlic cloves, crushed

1 fresh red chilli, deseeded
    and sliced

1 bunch spring onions, halved
    lengthways

125 ml/4 fl oz coconut milk

1 tsp chopped lemon grass

2 tsp lime juice

finely grated rind of 1 lime

1 tbsp chopped fresh coriander

COOK'S TIP

Make sure that you use a waxy
variety of potato that will keep
its shape when cooked. Check
that the potatoes are not
overcooked in step 2, otherwise
the potato pieces will
disintegrate when they are stir-
fried in the wok.

1 Using a sharp knife, cut the
potatoes into small cubes.

2 Bring a large saucepan of water
to the boil over a medium heat,
add the diced potatoes and cook for
5 minutes. Drain thoroughly.

3 Heat a wok or large, heavy-
based frying pan, add the
vegetable oil and heat, swirling the oil
around the base of the wok or pan
until it is really hot.

4 Add the potatoes, yellow and red
peppers, carrot, courgette, garlic
and chilli to the wok or pan and stir-fry
over a medium heat for 2–3 minutes.

5 Stir in the spring onions, coconut
milk, lemon grass and lime juice
and stir-fry the mixture for a further
5 minutes.

6 Add the lime rind and chopped
fresh coriander and stir-fry for
1 minute. Serve immediately while hot.

VARIATION

Before stir-frying the vegetables,
make an omelette garnish. Whisk
2 eggs with 2 tablespoons water,
3 tablespoons chopped fresh
coriander and seasoning. Heat 1
tablespoon of vegetable oil in
the wok and cook over a high
heat until the edges are crisp.
Flip over and cook the second
side for 30 seconds. Slide the
omelette on to a board and leave
to cool. Roll up loosely and cut
into thin slices.

Side Dishes

When the potato is thought of as a component of a meal, it is inevitably associated with meat and vegetables, and is served either roasted or  boiled. In fact, the potato is so versatile in its ability to combine with other flavourings and be cooked in so many different ways that it is the perfect base for a whole variety of delicious side dishes. This chapter demonstrates that versatility with a wide range of tantalizing recipes.

Potatoes can be cooked and served in many different ways, such as mashing, roasting, stir-frying, pan-frying, deep-frying, baking and boiling. You will find all kinds of different recipes for side dishes in this chapter, including Spanish Potatoes and Potatoes en Papillotes. There are also classic recipes, such as Potatoes Dauphinois and Pommes Anna, as well as updated versions of traditional dishes, such as Chilli Roast Potatoes and Spicy Potato Fries.

colcannon

serves four

225 g/8 oz green
   cabbage, shredded
5 tbsp milk
225 g/8 oz floury potatoes, diced
1 large leek, chopped
pinch of freshly grated nutmeg
1 tbsp butter, melted
salt and pepper

COOK'S TIP

There are many different varieties of cabbage, which produce hearts at varying times of year, so you can be sure of being able to make this delicious cabbage dish all year round.

1 Cook the shredded cabbage in a saucepan of lightly salted, boiling water for 7–10 minutes. Drain thoroughly and reserve.

2 Meanwhile, in a separate saucepan, bring the milk to the boil and add the potatoes and leek. Reduce the heat and simmer for 15–20 minutes, or until they are cooked through.

3 Stir in the grated nutmeg and thoroughly mash the potatoes and leek together.

4 Add the drained cabbage to the mashed potato and leek mixture and mix together well. Season to taste with salt and pepper.

5 Spoon the mixture into a warmed serving dish, making a hollow in the centre with the back of a spoon.

6 Carefully pour the melted butter into the hollow and serve the colcannon immediately.

spanish potatoes

serves four

2 tbsp olive oil

500 g/1 lb 2 oz small new
    potatoes, halved

1 onion, halved and sliced

1 green pepper, deseeded and
    cut into strips

1 tsp chilli powder

1 tsp prepared mustard

300 ml/10 fl oz passata

300 ml/10 fl oz vegetable stock

salt and pepper

chopped fresh parsley, to garnish

COOK'S TIP

In Spain, tapas are traditionally
served with a glass of chilled
sherry or some other aperitif.

1 Heat the olive oil in a large,
heavy-based frying pan. Add
the new potatoes and onion and cook
over a medium heat, stirring frequently,
for 4–5 minutes, until the onion slices
are soft and translucent.

2 Add the green pepper strips, chilli
powder and mustard to the pan
and cook for a further 2–3 minutes.

3 Stir the passata and the vegetable
stock into the pan and bring to
the boil. Reduce the heat and simmer
for about 25 minutes, or until the
potatoes are tender. Season to taste.

4 Transfer the potatoes to a
warmed serving dish. Sprinkle
the parsley over the top and serve
immediately. Alternatively, leave the
Spanish potatoes to cool completely
and serve at room temperature.

cheese crumble-topped mash

serves four

900 g/2 lb floury potatoes, diced

2 tbsp butter

2 tbsp milk

50 g/1¾ oz mature cheese or blue
cheese, grated

CRUMBLE TOPPING

3 tbsp butter

1 onion, cut into chunks

1 garlic clove, crushed

1 tbsp wholegrain mustard

175 g/ 6 oz fresh
wholemeal breadcrumbs

2 tbsp chopped fresh parsley

salt and pepper

VARIATION

Substitute natural yogurt for the
milk and Parmesan for Cheddar
cheese. Alternatively, omit the
cheese and stir in 200g/7 oz
chopped walnuts. Or substitute
young parsnips or celeriac for
half the potatoes. For a richer
texture use double cream instead
of milk.

1 Cook the potatoes in a pan of
boiling water for 10 minutes, or
until cooked through completely.

2 Meanwhile, make the crumble
topping. Melt the butter in a
frying pan. Add the onion, garlic and
wholegrain mustard and fry gently for
5 minutes, stirring constantly, until the
onion chunks have softened.

3 Put the breadcrumbs and parsley
in a mixing bowl and stir in the
fried onion mixture. Season to taste
with salt and pepper.

4 Drain the potatoes thoroughly
and place them in a mixing bowl.
Add the butter and milk, then mash
with a fork or potato masher until
smooth. Stir in the grated cheese while
the potato is still hot.

5 Spoon the mashed potato into
a shallow ovenproof dish and
sprinkle with the crumble topping.

6 Cook in a preheated oven,
200°C/400°F/Gas Mark 6, for
10–15 minutes, until the crumble
topping is golden brown and crunchy.
Serve immediately.

COOK'S TIP
For extra crunch, add freshly
cooked vegetables, such as
celery and peppers, to the
mashed potato in step 4.

potatoes en papillotes

serves four

450 g/1 lb small new potatoes

1 carrot, cut into matchsticks

1 fennel bulb, sliced

75 g/2¾ oz green beans

1 yellow pepper, deseeded and cut
    into strips

240 ml/8½ fl oz dry white wine

4 fresh rosemary sprigs

salt and pepper

fresh rosemary sprigs, to garnish

1 Cut 4 squares of greaseproof
paper measuring approximately
25-cm/10-inches in size.

2 Divide the vegetables equally
among the 4 paper squares,
placing them in the centre.

3 Bring the edges of the paper
together and scrunch them
together to encase the vegetables,
leaving the top open.

4 Place the parcels in a shallow
roasting tin and spoon
4 tablespoons of white wine into each
parcel. Add a rosemary sprig and
season to taste.

5 Fold the top of each parcel over
to seal it. Cook in a preheated
oven, 190°C/375°F/Gas Mark 5, for
30–35 minutes, or until the vegetables
are tender.

6 Transfer the sealed parcels to
four individual serving plates
and garnish with rosemary sprigs.

7 Open the parcels at the table in
order for the full aroma of the
vegetables to be appreciated.

COOK'S TIP

If small new potatoes are
unavailable, use larger potatoes
which have been halved or
quartered to ensure that they
cook through in the specified
cooking time.

gingered potatoes

serves four

675 g/1½ lb waxy potatoes, diced

2 tbsp vegetable oil

4 tsp grated fresh root ginger

1 fresh green chilli, deseeded
    and chopped

1 celery stick, chopped

25 g/1 oz cashew nuts

few saffron threads

3 tbsp boiling water

5 tbsp butter

celery leaves, to garnish

COOK'S TIP

Use a non-stick, heavy-based
frying pan because the potato
mixture is fairly dry and may stick
to an ordinary pan.

1 Cook the potatoes in a saucepan
of boiling water for 10 minutes,
then drain thoroughly.

2 Heat the oil in a heavy-based
frying pan and add the potatoes.
Cook over a medium heat, stirring
constantly, for about 3–4 minutes.

3 Add the grated ginger, chilli,
celery and cashew nuts and
cook for another minute.

4 Meanwhile, place the saffron
threads in a small bowl. Add the
boiling water and leave to soak for at
least 5 minutes.

5 Add the butter to the pan,
lower the heat and stir in the
saffron mixture. Cook over a low heat
for 10 minutes, or until the potatoes
are tender.

6 Transfer to a warm serving
dish, garnish the gingered
potatoes with the celery leaves
and serve at once.

trio of potato purées

serves four

1 tbsp butter, plus extra for greasing

300 g/10½ oz floury
    potatoes, chopped

125 g/4½ oz swede, chopped

1 carrot, chopped

450 g/1 lb fresh spinach

1 tbsp skimmed milk

2½ tbsp plain flour

1 egg

½ tsp ground cinnamon

1 tbsp orange juice

¼ tsp freshly grated nutmeg

salt and pepper

carrot matchsticks, to garnish

1 Lightly grease 4 x 150 ml/5 fl oz ramekins with butter.

2 Cook the potatoes in a saucepan of boiling water for 10 minutes. In separate pans cook the swede and carrot in boiling water for 10 minutes. Blanch the spinach in boiling water for 5 minutes. Drain the vegetables.

3 Add the milk and the tablespoon of butter to the potatoes and mash with a fork or potato masher until smooth. Stir in the flour and egg.

4 Divide the potato mixture among 3 medium-size bowls. Spoon the swede into one bowl and mix thoroughly. Spoon the carrot into the second bowl and mix thoroughly. Spoon the spinach into the third bowl and mix thoroughly.

5 Add the cinnamon to the swede and potato mixture and season to taste. Stir the orange juice into the carrot and potato mixture. Stir the grated nutmeg into the spinach and potato mixture.

6 Spoon a layer of the swede and potato mixture into each of the ramekins and smooth over the top. Cover each with a layer of spinach and potato mixture, then top with the carrot and potato mixture. Cover the ramekins with kitchen foil and place in a roasting tin. Half fill the tin with boiling water and cook in a preheated oven, 180°C/350°F/Gas Mark 4, for 40 minutes, or until set.

7 Turn out on to serving plates, garnish with the carrot matchsticks and serve immediately.

caramelized new potatoes

serves four

675 g/1½ lb new
   potatoes, scrubbed
4 tbsp dark brown sugar
55 g/2 oz butter
1 tbsp orange juice
1 tbsp chopped fresh parsley
   or coriander
salt and pepper
orange rind curls, to garnish

VARIATION

Lemon or lime juices may be
used instead of the orange juice,
if preferred. In addition, garnish
the finished dish with pared
lemon or lime rind, if desired.

1 Cook the new potatoes in a
saucepan of boiling water for
10 minutes, or until almost tender.
Drain thoroughly.

2 Melt all the sugar in a large,
heavy-based frying pan over
a low heat, stirring constantly.

3 Add the butter and orange juice
to the pan, stirring the mixture
constantly as the butter melts.

4 Add the potatoes to the orange
and butter mixture and continue
to cook, turning the potatoes
frequently until they are completely
coated in the caramel.

5 Sprinkle the chopped fresh parsley
or coriander over the potatoes
and season according to taste with salt
and pepper.

6 Transfer the caramelized new
potatoes to a warmed serving
dish and garnish with the orange rind.
Serve immediately.

spicy potatoes & onions

serves four

6 tbsp vegetable oil

2 onions, chopped finely

1 tsp finely chopped fresh
    root ginger

1 tsp crushed garlic

1 tsp chilli powder

1½ tsp ground cumin

1½ tsp ground coriander

1 tsp salt

400 g/14 oz canned new potatoes

1 tbsp lemon juice

BAGHAAR

3 tbsp oil

3 dried red chillies

½ tsp onion seeds

½ tsp mustard seeds

½ tsp fenugreek seeds

TO GARNISH

fresh coriander leaves

1 fresh green chilli, deseeded amd
    chopped finely

1 Heat the oil in a heavy-based pan. Cook the onions, stirring, until golden. Reduce the heat, add the ginger, garlic, chilli powder, ground cumin, ground coriander and salt and stir-fry for about 1 minute. Remove the pan from the heat and reserve.

2 Drain the water from the potatoes. Add the potatoes to the onion and spice mixture and heat through. Sprinkle over the lemon juice and mix well.

3 To make the baghaar, heat the oil in a separate pan. Add the red chillies, onion seeds, mustard seeds and fenugreek seeds and fry until the seeds turn a shade darker. Remove the pan from the heat and pour the baghaar over the potatoes.

4 Garnish with coriander leaves and chopped chilli, then serve.

121

spicy indian potatoes

serves four

½ tsp coriander seeds

1 tsp cumin seeds

4 tbsp vegetable oil

2 cardamom pods

1 tsp grated fresh root ginger

1 fresh red chilli, deseeded
  and chopped

1 onion, chopped

2 garlic cloves, crushed

450 g/1 lb new potatoes, quartered

150 ml/5 fl oz vegetable stock

675 g/1½ lb fresh spinach, chopped

4 tbsp natural yogurt

salt and pepper

VARIATION

Use frozen spinach instead
of fresh spinach, if you prefer.
Thaw the frozen spinach
and drain it thoroughly before
adding it to the dish, otherwise
it will turn soggy.

1 Grind the coriander and cumin
seeds using a pestle and mortar.

2 Heat the oil in a frying pan. Add
the ground coriander and cumin
seeds to the pan together with the
cardamom pods and ginger and cook
for about 2 minutes.

3 Add the chilli, onion and garlic
to the pan. Cook for a further
2 minutes, stirring frequently.

4 Add the potatoes to the pan
together with the vegetable stock.
Cook gently for 30 minutes, or until the
potatoes are cooked through, stirring
occasionally.

5 Add the spinach to the pan and
cook for a further 5 minutes.

6 Remove the pan from the heat
and stir in the yogurt. Season
with salt and pepper to taste. Transfer
the potatoes and spinach to a serving
dish and serve.

COOK'S TIP

An earthenware, marble or cast
iron mortar and pestle is ideal for
grinding spices. You can also buy
spice mills from kitchen shops,
but these are not always easy to
clean and you can end up with a
mixture of flavours that you do
not want.

potatoes in red wine

serves four

125 g/4½ oz butter

450 g/1 lb new potatoes, halved

200 ml/7 fl oz red wine

6 tbsp beef stock

8 shallots, halved

125 g/4½ oz oyster mushrooms

1 tbsp chopped fresh sage
   or coriander

salt and pepper

fresh sage leaves or coriander
   sprigs, to garnish

VARIATION

If oyster mushrooms are
unavailable, other mushrooms,
such as large open cap
mushrooms, can be used instead.

3 Stir in the mushrooms and
chopped herbs and cook for
5 minutes.

1 Melt the butter in a heavy-based
frying pan and add the potatoes.
Cook over a low heat for 5 minutes,
stirring constantly.

4 Turn the potatoes and
mushrooms into a warm serving
dish. Garnish with fresh sage leaves or
coriander sprigs and serve at once.

2 Add the red wine, beef stock
and shallots. Season to taste
with salt and pepper and simmer for
30 minutes.

pommes anna

serves four

5 tbsp butter, melted

675 g/1½ lb waxy potatoes

4 tbsp chopped mixed herbs

salt and pepper

chopped fresh herbs, to garnish

COOK'S TIP

Make sure that the potatoes are sliced very thinly so that they are almost transparent. This will ensure that they cook thoroughly.

1 Brush a shallow 1-litre/1¾-pint ovenproof dish with a little of the melted butter.

2 Slice the potatoes thinly and pat dry with kitchen paper.

3 Arrange a layer of potato slices in the prepared dish until the base is covered. Brush with a little butter and sprinkle with a quarter of the chopped mixed herbs. Season to taste.

4 Continue layering the potato slices, brushing each layer with melted butter and sprinkling with herbs, until they are all used up.

5 Brush the top layer of potato slices with butter, cover the dish and cook in a preheated oven, 190°C/375°F/Gas Mark 5, for 1½ hours.

6 Turn out on to a warm ovenproof platter and return to the oven for 25–30 minutes, until golden brown. Serve, garnished with fresh herbs.

125

grilled potatoes with lime

serves four

450 g/1 lb potatoes, unpeeled
and scrubbed

3 tbsp butter, melted

2 tbsp chopped fresh thyme

paprika, for dusting

salt and pepper

LIME MAYONNAISE

150 ml/5 fl oz mayonnaise

2 tsp lime juice

finely grated rind of 1 lime

1 garlic clove, crushed

pinch of paprika

salt and pepper

1 Cut the potatoes into 1-cm/
½-inch-thick slices.

2 Cook the potatoes in a saucepan
of boiling water for 5–7 minutes;
they should still be quite firm. Remove
the potatoes with a slotted spoon and
drain thoroughly.

3 Line a grill pan with kitchen foil.
Place the potato slices on top of
the foil.

4 Brush the potatoes with the
melted butter and sprinkle the
thyme on top. Season to taste with
salt and pepper.

5 Cook the potatoes under a
preheated medium grill, turning
once during cooking, for 10 minutes.

6 Meanwhile, make the lime
mayonnaise. In a small bowl,
combine the mayonnaise, lime juice,
lime rind, garlic, paprika and season
with salt and pepper to taste.

7 Transfer the hot potato slices to a
warmed serving dish and dust
them with a little paprika. Serve
immediately with the bowl of lime
mayonnaise for dipping.

COOK'S TIP

For an impressive side dish,
thread the potato slices on
to skewers and cook over
medium-hot barbecue coals.

potatoes dauphinois

serves four

1 tbsp butter

675 g/1½ lb waxy potatoes, sliced

2 garlic cloves, crushed

1 red onion, sliced

85 g/3 oz Gruyère cheese, grated

300 ml/10 fl oz double cream

salt and pepper

COOK'S TIP

There are many versions of
this classic potato dish, but the
different recipes always contain
double cream, making it a rich
and very filling side dish
or accompaniment.

1 Lightly grease a 1-litre/1¾-pint
shallow ovenproof dish with
the butter.

2 Arrange a single layer of potato
slices evenly in the base of the
prepared dish.

3 Top the potato slices with half
the garlic, half the sliced red
onion and one-third of the grated
Gruyère cheese. Season to taste with
a little salt and some pepper.

4 Repeat the layers in exactly the
same order, finishing with a layer
of potatoes topped with grated cheese.

5 Pour the cream over the top
of the potatoes and cook in a
preheated oven, 180°C/350°F/Gas
Mark 4, for 1½ hours, or until the
potatoes are cooked through and the
top is browned and crispy. Serve at
once, straight from the dish.

spicy potato fries

serves four

4 large waxy potatoes

2 sweet potatoes

4 tbsp butter, melted

½ tsp chilli powder

1 tsp garam masala

salt

COOK'S TIP

Rinsing the potatoes in cold water before cooking removes the starch, thus preventing them from sticking together. Soaking the potatoes in cold salted water makes the cooked chips crisper.

1 Cut both the potatoes and sweet potatoes into slices about 1-cm/ ½-inch thick, then cut them into finger-shaped chips.

2 Place the potatoes in a large bowl of cold salted water. Leave to soak for 20 minutes.

3 Remove the potato slices with a slotted spoon and drain thoroughly. Pat with kitchen paper until they are completely dry.

4 Pour the melted butter on to a baking tray. Transfer the potato slices to the baking tray.

5 Sprinkle with the chilli powder and garam masala, turning the potato slices to coat them with the spice mixture.

6 Cook the chips in a preheated oven, 200°C/400°F/Gas Mark 6, turning frequently, for 40 minutes, until browned and cooked through.

7 Drain the fries well on kitchen paper to remove the excess oil and serve immediately.

lemony & herby potatoes

serves four

LEMONY NEW POTATOES

1 kg/2 lb 4 oz new potatoes

25 g/1 oz butter

1 tbsp zested lemon rind

2 tbsp lemon juice

1 tbsp chopped fresh dill or chives

salt and pepper

extra chopped fresh dill or chives,
   to garnish

HERBY NEW POTATOES

1 kg/2 lb 4 oz new potatoes

3 tbsp light olive oil

1 tbsp white wine vinegar

pinch of dry mustard

pinch of caster sugar

2 tbsp chopped mixed fresh herbs,
   such as parsley, chives,
   marjoram, basil and rosemary

salt and pepper

fresh mixed herbs sprigs,
   to garnish

1 For the lemony potatoes, either scrub the potatoes well or remove the skins by scraping them off with the blade of a sharp knife. Cook the potatoes in plenty of lightly salted, boiling water for about 15 minutes, until just tender.

2 While the potatoes are cooking, melt the butter over a low heat. Add the lemon rind, juice and herbs. Season with salt and pepper.

3 Drain the cooked potatoes and transfer to a serving bowl.

4 Pour over the lemony butter mixture and stir gently to mix. Garnish with extra herbs and serve hot or warm.

5 For the herby potatoes, prepare and cook the potatoes as described in step 1. Whisk the olive oil, vinegar, mustard, caster sugar and seasoning together in a small bowl. Add the chopped herbs and mix well.

6 Drain the potatoes and pour over the oil and vinegar mixture, stirring to coat evenly. Garnish with extra fresh herbs and serve warm or cold.

potatoes lyonnaise

serves six

1.25 kg/2 lb 12 oz potatoes

4 tbsp olive oil

2 tbsp butter

2 onions, sliced

2–3 garlic cloves, crushed (optional)

salt and pepper

chopped fresh parsley, to garnish

COOK'S TIP

If the potatoes blacken slightly
as they are boiling, add a
spoonful of lemon juice to
the cooking water.

1 Cut the potatoes into 5-mm/ ¼-inch slices. Put in a large saucepan of lightly salted water and bring to the boil. Cover and simmer gently for about 10–12 minutes, until just tender. Avoid boiling too rapidly or the potatoes will break up and lose their shape. When cooked, drain well.

2 While the potatoes are cooking, heat the oil and butter in a very large frying pan. Add the onions and garlic, if using, and fry over a medium heat, stirring frequently, until the onions are softened.

3 Add the cooked potato to the frying pan and cook with the onions, stirring occasionally, for about 5–8 minutes, until the potatoes are well browned.

4 Season to taste with salt and pepper. Sprinkle over the chopped parsley to serve. If wished, transfer the potatoes and onions to a large ovenproof dish and keep warm in a low oven until ready to serve.

potatoes in creamed coconut

serves four

600 g/1 lb 5 oz potatoes

1 onion, sliced thinly

2 fresh red bird-eye chillies,
    deseeded and chopped finely

½ tsp salt

½ tsp ground black pepper

85 g/3 oz creamed coconut

350 ml/12 fl oz vegetable or chicken
    stock

chopped fresh coriander or basil,
    to garnish

COOK'S TIP

If the potatoes are thin-skinned, or are new potatoes, simply wash or scrub to remove any dirt and cook with the skins on. This adds extra dietary fibre and nutrients to the finished dish, and cuts down on the preparation time. Baby new potatoes can be cooked whole.

1 Peel the potatoes thinly. Use a sharp knife to cut into 2-cm/ ¾-inch chunks.

2 Place the potatoes in a pan with the onion, bird-eye chillies, salt, pepper and creamed coconut. Stir in the stock.

3 Bring to the boil, stirring, then lower the heat, cover the pan and simmer gently, stirring occasionally, until the potatoes are tender.

4 Adjust the seasoning to taste, then sprinkle with chopped coriander or basil. Serve immediately while hot.

potatoes in green sauce

serves five

1 kg/2 lb 4 oz small waxy
potatoes, peeled

1 onion, halved and unpeeled

8 garlic cloves, unpeeled

1 fresh green chilli

8 tomatillos, outer husks removed,
or small tart tomatoes

225 ml/8 fl oz chicken, meat or
vegetable stock

1 tsp ground cumin

1 fresh thyme sprig or generous
pinch of dried thyme

1 fresh oregano sprig or generous
pinch of dried oregano

2 tbsp vegetable or extra virgin
olive oil

1 courgette, chopped roughly

1 bunch of fresh coriander, chopped

salt

1 Put the potatoes in a pan of
salted water. Bring to the boil
and cook for about 15 minutes, or until
almost tender. Do not overcook them.
Drain and reserve.

2 Meanwhile lightly char the onion,
garlic, chilli and tomatillos or
tomatoes in a heavy-based, ungreased
frying pan. Reserve, and when cool
enough to handle, peel and chop the
onion, garlic and chilli; chop the
tomatillos or tomatoes. Put in a
blender or food processor with half
the stock and process to form a purée.
Add the cumin, thyme and oregano.

3 Heat the oil in the heavy-based
frying pan. Add the purée and
cook for 5 minutes, stirring, to reduce
slightly and concentrate the flavours.

4 Add the potatoes and courgette
to the purée and pour in the
remainder of the stock. Add about half
of the coriander and cook over a low
heat for a further 5 minutes, or until
the courgette is tender.

5 Transfer to a serving bowl
and serve immediately, sprinkled
with the remaining chopped coriander
to garnish.

potatoes with almonds

serves four

600 g/1 lb 5 oz potatoes, unpeeled
    and sliced

1 tbsp vegetable oil

1 red onion, halved and sliced

1 garlic clove, crushed

50 g/1¾ oz flaked almond

½ tsp ground turmeric

125 g/4½ oz rocket leaves

300ml/10 fl oz double cream

salt and pepper

1 Cook the sliced potatoes in a saucepan of boiling water for 10 minutes. Drain thoroughly.

2 Heat the vegetable oil in a heavy-based frying pan. Add the onion and garlic and fry over a medium heat, stirring frequently, for 3–4 minutes.

3 Add the almonds, turmeric and potato slices to the frying pan and cook, stirring constantly, for 2–3 minutes. Stir in the rocket.

4 Transfer the potato and almond mixture to a shallow ovenproof dish. Pour the double cream over the top and season with salt and pepper.

5 Cook in a preheated oven, 190°C/375°F/Gas Mark 5, for about 20 minutes, or until the potatoes are cooked through. Transfer to a warmed serving dish and serve immediately.

potato & mushroom bake

serves four

2 tbsp butter

500 g/1 lb 2 oz waxy potatoes,
    sliced thinly

150 g/5½ oz sliced
    mixed mushrooms

1 tbsp chopped fresh rosemary

4 tbsp snipped fresh chives

2 garlic cloves, crushed

150 ml/5 fl oz double cream

salt and pepper

snipped fresh chives, to garnish

1 Grease a shallow round
ovenproof dish with the butter.

2 Parboil the potatoes in a
saucepan of boiling water for
10 minutes. Drain well. Layer a quarter
of the potatoes in the base of the dish.

3 Arrange one-quarter of the
mushrooms on top of the
potatoes and sprinkle with one-quarter
of the rosemary, chives and garlic.
Continue making layers in the same
order, finishing with a layer of potatoes
on top.

4 Pour the cream over the top of
the potatoes. Season to taste with
salt and pepper.

5 Cook in a preheated oven, 190°C/
375°F/Gas Mark 5, for about
45 minutes, or until the bake is golden
brown and piping hot.

6 Garnish with snipped fresh chives
and serve immediately, straight
from the dish.

cheese & potato slices

COOK'S TIP

The cheese and potato slices may
be coated in the breadcrumb
mixture in advance and then
stored in the refrigerator until
ready to use.

1 Cook the potatoes in a saucepan of boiling water for about 10–15 minutes, or until the potatoes are just tender. Drain thoroughly.

2 Mix the breadcrumbs, cheese and chilli powder together in a bowl, then transfer to a shallow dish. Pour the beaten eggs into a separate shallow dish.

3 Dip the potato slices first in egg and then roll them in the breadcrumbs to coat completely.

4 Heat the oil in a large saucepan or deep-fryer to 180–190°C/ 350–375°F or until a cube of bread browns in 30 seconds. Cook the cheese and potato slices, in several batches, for 4–5 minutes or until a golden brown colour.

5 Remove the cheese and potato slices from the oil with a slotted spoon and drain thoroughly on kitchen paper. Keep the cheese and potato slices warm while you cook the remaining batches.

6 Transfer the cheese and potato slices to warm individual serving plates. Dust lightly with chilli powder, if using, and serve immediately.

fried potatoes with onions

serves four

900 g/2 lb waxy potatoes, diced

125 g/4½ oz butter

1 red onion, cut into 8 wedges

2 garlic cloves, crushed

1 tsp lemon juice

2 tbsp chopped fresh thyme

salt and pepper

1 Cook the diced potatoes in a saucepan of boiling water for 10 minutes. Drain thoroughly.

2 Melt the butter in a large, heavy-based frying pan and add the red onion wedges, garlic and lemon juice. Cook for 2–3 minutes, stirring.

3 Add the potatoes to the pan and mix well to coat in the butter mixture.

4 Reduce the heat, cover the frying pan with a lid or foil and cook for 25–30 minutes, or until the potatoes are golden and tender.

5 Sprinkle the chopped thyme over the top of the potatoes and season with salt and pepper to taste.

6 Serve immediately as a side dish to accompany grilled meats or fish.

spiced potatoes & spinach

serves four

3 tbsp vegetable oil

1 red onion, sliced

2 garlic cloves, crushed

½ tsp chilli powder

2 tsp ground coriander

1 tsp ground cumin

150 ml/5 fl oz vegetable stock

300 g/10½ oz potatoes, diced

500 g/1 lb 2 oz baby spinach

1 fresh red chilli, deseeded
    and sliced

salt and pepper

1 Heat the oil in a heavy-based frying pan. Add the onion and garlic and sauté over a medium heat, stirring occasionally, for 2–3 minutes.

2 Stir in the chilli powder, ground coriander and cumin and cook, stirring constantly, for a further 30 seconds.

COOK'S TIP

Besides adding extra colour
to a dish, red onions have a
sweeter, less pungent flavour
than other varieties.

3 Add the vegetable stock, potatoes and spinach and bring to the boil. Reduce the heat, cover the frying pan and simmer for about 10 minutes, or until the potatoes are cooked through and tender.

4 Uncover the pan, season to taste with salt and pepper, add the chilli and cook, stirring occasionally, for a further 2–3 minutes. Transfer to a warmed serving dish and serve the spiced potatoes immediately.

potatoes, olives & anchovies

serves four

450 g/1 lb baby new
    potatoes, scrubbed
85 g/3 oz mixed olives
8 canned anchovy fillets, drained
    and chopped
2 tbsp olive oil
2 fennel bulbs, trimmed and sliced
2 fresh rosemary sprigs,
    stalks removed
salt

COOK'S TIP

Fresh rosemary is particularly
popular with Italians, but you
can experiment with your
favourite herbs in this recipe,
if you prefer.

1 Bring a large pan of lightly salted water to the boil. Add the potatoes, bring back to the boil and simmer over a medium heat for 8–10 minutes, or until tender. Remove the potatoes from the pan using a slotted spoon and leave to cool.

2 Once the potatoes are cool enough to handle, cut them into wedges, using a sharp knife.

3 Stone the mixed olives with a cherry stoner or small, sharp knife and cut them in half.

4 Using a sharp knife, chop the anchovy fillets into thinner strips.

5 Heat the olive oil in a large, heavy-based frying pan. Add the potato wedges, sliced fennel and rosemary. Cook over a medium heat, gently stirring occasionally, for 7–8 minutes, or until the potatoes are golden brown.

6 Stir in the olives and anchovies and cook for 1 minute, or until completely warmed through.

7 Transfer the potato mixture to warmed individual serving plates and serve immediately.

italian potato wedges

serves four

2 large waxy potatoes, unpeeled

4 large ripe tomatoes, skinned
and deseeded

150 ml/5 fl oz vegetable stock

2 tbsp tomato purée

1 small yellow pepper, deseeded
and cut into strips

125 g/4½ oz button
mushrooms, quartered

1 tbsp chopped fresh basil

50 g/1¾ oz cheese, grated

salt and pepper

1 Cut each of the potatoes into 8 equal wedges. Parboil the potatoes in a pan of boiling water for 15 minutes. Drain well and place in a shallow ovenproof dish.

2 Chop the tomatoes and add them to the dish. Mix together the vegetable stock and tomato purée in a jug, then pour the mixture over the potatoes and tomatoes.

3 Add the yellow pepper strips, mushrooms and chopped basil to the dish. Season to taste with salt and pepper.

4 Sprinkle the grated cheese evenly over the top and cook in a preheated oven, 190°C/375°F/Gas Mark 5, for 15–20 minutes, until the topping is golden brown and bubbling. Serve the potato wedges immediately, straight from the dish.

potatoes with goat's cheese

serves four

1.25 kg/2 lb 12 oz baking potatoes,
    peeled and cut into chunks

pinch of salt

pinch of sugar

200 ml/7 fl oz crème fraîche

125 ml/4 fl oz vegetable or
    chicken stock

3 garlic cloves, chopped finely

a few shakes of bottled chipotle
    salsa, or 1 dried chipotle chilli,
    rehydrated, deseeded and
    sliced thinly

225 g/8 oz goat's cheese, sliced

175 g/6 oz mozzarella or Cheddar
    cheese, grated

50 g/1¾ oz Parmesan or pecorino
    cheese, grated

1 Put the potatoes in a large pan of water and add the salt and sugar. Bring to the boil, lower the heat and cook for about 10 minutes, until they are half cooked. Drain thoroughly and leave on the side.

2 Combine the crème fraîche with the stock, garlic and chipotle salsa or rehydrated dried chipotle chilli in a small bowl.

3 Arrange half the potatoes in a casserole. Pour half the crème fraîche sauce over the potatoes and cover with the goat's cheese. Top with the remaining potatoes and the sauce.

4 Sprinkle with the grated mozzarella or Cheddar cheese, then with either the grated Parmesan or pecorino cheese.

5 Bake in a preheated oven, 180°C/ 350°F/Gas Mark 4, for about 25 minutes, until the potatoes are tender and the cheese topping is lightly golden and has become crisp in places. Serve immediately.

souffléed cheesy potato fries

serves four

900 g/2 lb potatoes, cut into chunks

150 ml/5 fl oz double cream

75 g/2¾ oz Gruyère cheese, grated

pinch of cayenne pepper

2 egg whites

vegetable oil, for deep-frying

salt and pepper

TO GARNISH

chopped fresh flat-leaved parsley

grated cheese

VARIATION

Add other flavourings, such as grated nutmeg or curry powder, to the cream and cheese.

COOK'S TIP

Gruyère cheese has a sweet, nutty flavour and melts well. Look for the genuine product, which will have 'Switzerland' stamped all over the rind. It should have only a sprinkling of small holes.

1 Cook the potatoes in a saucepan of lightly salted, boiling water for about 10 minutes. Drain thoroughly and pat dry with absorbent kitchen paper. Leave until required.

2 Mix the double cream and Gruyère cheese in a large bowl. Stir in the cayenne pepper and season with salt and pepper to taste.

3 Whisk the egg whites until stiff peaks form. Gently fold into the cheese mixture until fully incorporated.

4 Add the cooked potatoes, turning to coat thoroughly in the mixture.

5 Heat the oil for deep-frying to 180–190°C/350–375°F or until a cube of bread browns in 30 seconds. Remove the potatoes from the cheese mixture with a slotted spoon and cook in the oil, in batches if necessary, for 3–4 minutes, or until golden.

6 Transfer the potatoes to a warmed serving dish and garnish with parsley and grated cheese. Serve the fries immediately.

chilli roast potatoes

serves four

500 g/1 lb 2 oz small new
    potatoes, scrubbed
150 ml/5 fl oz vegetable oil
1 tsp chilli powder
½ tsp caraway seeds
1 tsp salt
1 tbsp chopped fresh basil

VARIATION

Use any other spice of your
choice, such as curry powder or
paprika, for a variation in flavour.

1 Cook the potatoes in a saucepan of boiling water for 10 minutes, then drain thoroughly.

2 Pour a little of the oil into a shallow roasting tin to coat the base. Heat the oil in a preheated oven, 200°C/ 400°F/Gas Mark 6, for 10 minutes. Add the potatoes to the tin and brush them with the hot oil.

3 In a small bowl, mix together the chilli powder, caraway seeds and salt. Sprinkle the mixture over the potatoes, turning to coat them all over.

4 Add the remaining oil to the tin and roast in the oven for about 15 minutes, or until the potatoes are cooked through.

5 Using a slotted spoon, remove the potatoes from the the oil, draining them thoroughly, and transfer them to a warmed serving dish. Sprinkle the chopped basil over the top and serve immediately.

parmesan potatoes

serves four

1.3 kg/3 lb potatoes

50 g/1¾ oz Parmesan cheese,
freshly grated

pinch of freshly grated nutmeg

1 tbsp chopped fresh parsley

vegetable oil, for roasting

4 smoked bacon slices, cut
into strips

salt

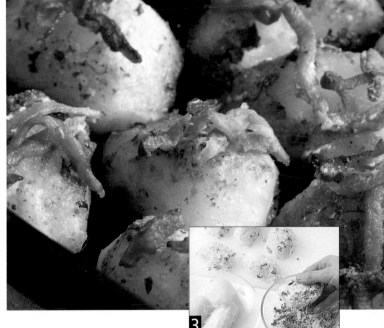

1 Cut the potatoes in half lengthways and cook them in a saucepan of salted, boiling water for 10 minutes. Drain thoroughly.

2 Mix the Parmesan, nutmeg and parsley together in a bowl.

3 Roll the potato pieces in the cheese mixture to coat them completely. Shake off any excess.

4 Pour a little oil into a roasting tin and then heat it in a preheated oven, 200°C/400°F/Gas Mark 6, for 10 minutes. Remove from the oven and put the potatoes into the tin. Return the potatoes to the oven and cook for 30 minutes, turning once.

5 Remove from the oven and sprinkle the bacon on top of the potatoes. Return to the oven for 15 minutes, or until the potatoes and bacon are cooked. Drain off any excess fat and serve.

VARIATION

If you prefer, use slices of salami or Parma ham instead of the bacon, adding it to the dish 5 minutes before the end of the cooking time.

149

mini vegetable puff pastries

serves four

PASTRY CASES

450 g/1 lb puff pastry, thawed
    if frozen

1 egg, beaten

FILLING

225 g/8 oz sweet potatoes, diced

100 g/3½ oz baby asparagus spears

2 tbsp butter or margarine

1 leek, sliced

2 small open-cap mushrooms, sliced

1 tsp lime juice

1 tsp chopped fresh thyme

pinch of mustard powder

salt and pepper

COOK'S TIP

Making puff pastry yourself is not difficult, but is immensely time-consuming because it involves a process of rolling, folding and chilling that is repeated several times. Ready-made puff pastry, either frozen or chilled, is usually of good quality and is certainly more convenient for the busy cook.

1 Cut the pastry into 4 equal pieces. Roll each piece out on a lightly floured work surface to form a 13-cm/5-inch square. Place on a dampened baking tray and score a smaller 6-cm/2½-inch square inside.

2 Brush with beaten egg and cook in a preheated oven, 200°C/400°F/Gas Mark 6, for 20 minutes or until risen and golden brown.

VARIATION

Use a colourful selection of any vegetables you have to hand for this recipe.

3 While the pastry is cooking, start the filling. Cook the sweet potato in boiling water for 15 minutes, then drain. Blanch the asparagus in boiling water for 10 minutes or until tender. Drain and reserve.

4 Remove the pastry squares from the oven. Carefully cut out the central square of pastry, lift it out and reserve.

5 Melt the butter or margarine in a pan and sauté the leek and mushrooms for 2–3 minutes. Add the lime juice, thyme and mustard, season well and stir in the sweet potatoes and asparagus. Spoon into the pastry cases, top with the reserved pastry squares and serve immediately

pesto potatoes

serves four

900 g/2 lb small new potatoes

75 g/2¾ oz fresh basil

2 tbsp pine kernels

3 garlic cloves, crushed

100 ml/3½ fl oz olive oil

75 g/2¾ oz mixed Parmesan cheese
   and pecorino cheese, grated

salt and pepper

fresh basil sprigs, to garnish

1 Cook the potatoes in a saucepan of boiling salted water for 15 minutes, or until tender. Drain well, transfer to a warm serving dish and keep warm until required.

2 Meanwhile, put the basil, pine kernels, garlic and a little salt and pepper to taste in a food processor. Blend for 30 seconds, then add the oil gradually, processing until smooth.

3 Remove the mixture from the food processor and transfer it to a mixing bowl. Stir in the grated Parmesan and pecorino cheeses.

4 Spoon the pesto sauce over the warm potatoes and mix well. Garnish with fresh basil sprigs and serve immediately.

bombay potatoes

serves four

1 kg/2 lb 4 oz waxy potatoes

2 tbsp vegetable ghee

1 tsp panch poran spice mix 3 tsp
    ground turmeric

2 tbsp tomato purée

300 ml/10 fl oz natural yogurt

salt

chopped fresh coriander, to garnish

COOK'S TIP

For panch poran spice, mix
equal quantities of cumin, fennel,
mustard, nigella and fenugreek
seeds.

1 Put the whole potatoes into a
large saucepan of salted cold
water, bring to the boil, then simmer
until the potatoes are just cooked, but
not tender; the time depends on the
size of the potato, but an average-size
one should take about 15 minutes.

2 Heat the ghee in a separate
saucepan over a medium heat
and add the spices, tomato purée,
yogurt and salt. Bring to the boil, and
simmer, uncovered, for 5 minutes.

3 Drain the potatoes and cut each
one into 4 pieces. Add the
potatoes to the pan, cover and cook
briefly. Transfer to an ovenproof
casserole, cover and cook in a
preheated oven, 180°C/350°F/Gas
Mark 4, for about 40 minutes, or until
the potatoes are tender and the sauce
has thickened a little.

4 Sprinkle with chopped coriander
and serve immediately.

153

crispy potato skins

serves four

8 small baking potatoes, scrubbed

4 tbsp butter, melted

salt and pepper

OPTIONAL TOPPING

6 spring onions, sliced

50 g/1¾ oz Gruyère cheese, grated

50 g/1¾ oz salami, cut into
   thin strips

COOK'S TIP

Potato skins can be served on
their own, but they are delicious
served with a dip. Try a spicy
tomato or hummus dip.

1 Prick the potatoes with a fork and bake in a preheated oven, 200°C/400°F/Gas Mark 6, for about 1 hour, or until tender.

2 Cut the potatoes in half and scoop out the flesh with a teaspoon, leaving about 5-mm/¼-inch potato flesh lining the skin. Be careful not to pierce the skins.

3 Brush the insides of the potato with melted butter.

4 Place the skins, cut-side down, over medium hot coals and cook for 10–15 minutes. Alternatively, cook under a preheated grill.

5 Turn the potato skins over and cook for a further 5 minutes or until they are crispy. Take care that they do not burn.

6 Season the potato skins with salt and pepper to taste and serve while they are still warm.

7 If wished, the skins can be filled with a variety of toppings. Barbecue (or grill) the potato skins as above for about 10 minutes, then turn cut side up and sprinkle with slices of spring onion, grated cheese and salami strips. Cook on the barbecue or grill for a further 5 minutes, until the cheese begins to melt. Serve hot.

paprika crisps

serves four

2 large potatoes

3 tbsp olive oil

½ tsp paprika

salt

1 Slice the potatoes very thinly so that they are almost transparent and place in a bowl of cold water. Drain the potato slices thoroughly and pat dry with kitchen paper.

2 Heat the oil in a large, heavy-based frying pan and add the paprika. Cook, stirring constantly to ensure that the paprika doesn't catch on the base and burn.

3 Add the potato slices to the frying pan and cook them in a single layer over a medium-low heat for about 5 minutes, or until the potato slices are just beginning to curl slightly at the edges.

4 Remove the potato slices from the pan using a slotted spoon and transfer them to kitchen paper to drain thoroughly.

5 Thread the potato slices on to several wooden kebab skewers.

6 Sprinkle the potato slices with salt and cook over a medium hot barbecue or under a medium grill, turning frequently, for 10 minutes, until they begin to go crisp. Sprinkle with a little more salt and serve immediately.

chinese potato crisps

serves four

650 g/1 lb 7 oz medium potatoes

125 ml/4 fl oz vegetable oil

1 fresh red chilli, halved
    and deseeded

1 small onion, quartered

2 garlic cloves, halved

2 tbsp light soy sauce

pinch of salt

1 tsp wine vinegar

1 tbsp coarse sea salt

pinch of chilli powder

1 Peel the potatoes and cut into thin slices along their length. Cut the slices into matchsticks.

2 Bring a saucepan of water to the boil and blanch the potato sticks for 2 minutes, drain, rinse under cold water and drain well again. Pat the potato sticks thoroughly dry with absorbent kitchen paper.

3 Heat the oil in a preheated wok until it is almost smoking. Add the chilli, onion and garlic and stir-fry for 30 seconds. Remove and discard the chilli, onion and garlic.

4 Add the potato sticks to the oil and fry for 3–4 minutes, or until golden all over.

5 Add the soy sauce, salt and vinegar to the wok, reduce the heat and cook for 1 minute, or until the potatoes are crisp.

6 Remove the potatoes with a slotted spoon and drain on absorbent kitchen paper.

7 Transfer the potato sticks to a serving dish, sprinkle with the sea salt and chilli powder and serve.

garlic potato wedges

serves four

3 large baking potatoes, scrubbed

4 tbsp olive oil

2 tbsp butter

2 garlic cloves, chopped

1 tbsp chopped fresh rosemary

1 tbsp chopped fresh parsley

1 tbsp chopped fresh thyme

salt and pepper

COOK'S TIP

You may find it easier to barbecue these potatoes in a hinged rack.

1 Bring a large pan of water to the boil, add the potatoes and parboil them for 10 minutes. Drain the potatoes, refresh under cold water and then drain them again thoroughly.

2 Transfer the potatoes to a chopping board. When the potatoes are cold enough to handle, cut them into thick wedges, but do not peel.

3 Heat the oil and butter in a small pan together with the garlic. Cook gently until the garlic begins to brown, then remove the pan from the heat.

4 Stir the herbs and seasoning into the mixture in the pan.

5 Brush the herb and butter mixture all over the potato wedges.

6 Barbecue the potatoes over hot coals for 10–15 minutes, brushing liberally with any of the remaining herb and butter mixture, or until the potato wedges are just tender. Alternatively, cook under the grill.

7 Transfer the garlic potato wedges to a warm serving plate and serve as a starter or as a side dish.

Meat & Poultry

This chapter contains a wide selection of delicious main meal dishes. The potato is the main ingredient in the majority of these recipes, but there are also ideas for adding meat, poultry, fish and vegetables, so that there is sure to be something for everyone. The recipes come from all around the world – try Potato Ravioli or Lamb & Potato Masal. There are also hearty dishes, including creamy Chicken & Potato Casserole, and Shepherd's Pie. Whatever the occasion, you are sure to find something here to entice you.

potato ravioli

serves four

FILLING

1 tbsp vegetable oil

125 g/4½ oz fresh beef mince

1 shallot, diced

1 garlic clove, crushed

1 tbsp plain flour

1 tbsp tomato purée

150 ml/5 fl oz beef stock

1 celery stick, chopped

2 tomatoes, skinned and diced

2 tsp chopped fresh basil

salt and pepper

RAVIOLI

450 g/1 lb floury potatoes, diced

3 small egg yolks

3 tbsp olive oil

175 g/6 oz plain flour, plus extra
   for dusting

5 tbsp butter, for frying

salt and pepper

shredded basil leaves, to garnish

1 To make the filling, heat the oil in a pan and fry the beef for 3–4 minutes, breaking it up with a spoon. Add the shallot and garlic and cook for 2–3 minutes, until the shallot has softened.

2 Stir in the flour and tomato purée and cook for 1 minute. Stir in the beef stock, celery, tomatoes and chopped fresh basil. Season to taste with salt and pepper.

3 Cook the mixture over a low heat for 20 minutes. Remove from the heat and leave to cool.

4 To make the ravioli, cook the potatoes in a pan of boiling water for 10 minutes, until tender.

5 Mash the potatoes and place them in a mixing bowl. Blend in the egg yolks and oil. Season with salt and pepper, then stir in the flour and mix to form a dough.

6 On a lightly floured surface, divide the dough into 24 pieces and shape into flat rounds. Spoon the filling on to one half of each round and fold the dough over to encase the filling, pressing down firmly to seal the edges.

7 Melt the butter in a frying pan and cook the ravioli in batches for 6–8 minutes, turning once, until golden. Serve hot, garnished with chopped fresh basil leaves.

potato, beef & peanut pot

serves four

1 tbsp vegetable oil

5 tbsp butter

450 g/1 lb lean beef steak, cut into
thin strips

1 onion, halved and sliced

2 garlic cloves, crushed

600 g/1 lb 5 oz waxy
potatoes, diced

½ tsp paprika

4 tbsp crunchy peanut butter

600 ml/1 pint beef stock

25 g/1 oz unsalted peanuts

2 tsp light soy sauce

50 g/1¼ oz sugar snap peas

1 red pepper, deseeded and cut
into strips

fresh parsley sprigs, to garnish

1 Heat the oil and butter in a
flameproof casserole.

2 Add the beef strips and fry them
gently for 3–4 minutes, stirring
and turning the meat until it is sealed
on all sides.

3 Add the onion and garlic and
cook for a further 2 minutes,
stirring constantly.

4 Add the diced potatoes and cook
for 3–4 minutes, or until they
begin to brown slightly.

5 Stir in the paprika and peanut
butter, then gradually blend in the
beef stock. Bring the mixture to the
boil, stirring frequently.

6 Finally, add the peanuts, soy sauce,
sugar snap peas and red pepper.

7 Cover and cook over a low heat
for 45 minutes, or until the beef is
cooked right through.

8 Garnish the potato, beef and
peanut pot with fresh parsley if
liked, and serve immediately.

potato & meat filo packets

serves four

225 g/8 oz waxy potatoes,
   finely diced

1 tbsp vegetable oil

115 g/4 oz fresh beef mince

1 leek, sliced

1 small yellow pepper, deseeded
   and finely diced

115 g/4 oz button
   mushrooms, sliced

1 tbsp plain flour

1 tbsp tomato purée

6 tbsp red wine

6 tbsp beef stock

1 tbsp chopped fresh rosemary

225 g/8 oz filo pastry, thawed
   if frozen

2 tbsp butter, melted

salt and pepper

1 Cook the diced potatoes in a saucepan of boiling water for 5 minutes. Drain and reserve.

2 Meanwhile, heat the oil in a saucepan and fry the beef mince, leek, yellow pepper and mushrooms over a low heat for 5 minutes.

3 Stir in the flour and tomato purée and cook for 1 minute. Gradually add the red wine and beef stock, stir until thickened. Add the chopped rosemary, season to taste with salt and pepper and leave to cool slightly.

4 Lay 4 sheets of filo pastry on a work surface or board. Brush each sheet with butter and lay a second layer of filo on top. Trim the sheets to make 4 x 20-cm/8-inch squares.

5 Brush the edges of the pastry with a little butter. Spoon a quarter of the beef mixture into the centre of each square. Bring up the corners and the sides of the squares to form a parcel, scrunching the edges together. Make sure that the parcels are well sealed by pressing the pastry together, otherwise the filling will leak.

6 Place the parcels on a baking sheet and brush with butter. Bake in a preheated oven, 180°C/350°F/Gas Mark 4, for 20 minutes. Serve hot.

potato, beef & kidney pie

serves four

225 g/8 oz waxy potatoes, diced

2 tbsp butter

450 g/1 lb lean beef steak, diced

150 g/5½ oz ox kidney, cored
   and chopped

12 shallots

1 tbsp plain flour, plus extra
   for dusting

150 ml/5 fl oz beef stock

150 ml/5 fl oz stout

225 g/8 oz ready-made puff pastry,
   thawed if frozen

1 egg, beaten

salt and pepper

1 Cook the diced potatoes in a saucepan of boiling water for 10 minutes. Drain thoroughly.

2 Meanwhile, melt the butter in a saucepan and add the diced steak and the chopped kidney. Cook, stirring constantly, for 5 minutes, until the meat is sealed on all sides.

3 Add the shallots and cook for a further 3–4 minutes. Stir in the flour and cook for 1 minute. Gradually stir in the beef stock and stout and bring to the boil, stirring constantly.

4 Stir the potatoes into the meat mixture and season with salt and pepper. Reduce the heat until the mixture is simmering. Cover the saucepan with a lid and cook for 1 hour, stirring occasionally.

5 Spoon the beef mixture into the base of a pie dish. Roll out the pastry on a lightly floured surface until it is 1-cm/½-inch larger than the top of the dish.

6 Cut a strip of pastry long enough and wide enough to fit around the edge of the dish. Brush the edge of the dish with beaten egg and press the pastry strip around the edge. Brush with egg and place the pastry lid on top. Crimp to seal the edge and knock up the rim with the back of a knife blade. Brush with beaten egg.

7 Cook in a preheated oven, 230°C/450°F/Gas Mark 8, for 20–25 minutes, or until the pastry has risen and is golden brown. Serve the pie immediately, while it is hot, straight from the dish.

carrot-topped beef pie

serves four

450 g/1 lb lean fresh beef mince

1 onion, chopped

1 garlic clove, crushed

1 tbsp plain flour

300 ml/10 fl oz beef stock

2 tbsp tomato purée

1 celery stick, chopped

3 tbsp chopped fresh parsley

1 tbsp Worcestershire sauce

675 g/1½ lb floury potatoes, diced

2 large carrots, diced

2 tbsp butter

3 tbsp skimmed milk

salt and pepper

1 Dry-fry the beef in a large pan set over a high heat for 3–4 minutes, or until sealed. Add the onion and garlic and cook for a further 5 minutes, stirring.

2 Add the flour and cook for 1 minute. Gradually blend in the beef stock and tomato purée. Stir in the celery, 1 tablespoon of the parsley and the Worcestershire sauce. Season to taste.

3 Bring the mixture to the boil, then reduce the heat and simmer for 20–25 minutes. Spoon the beef mixture into a 1.2-litre/ 2-pint pie dish.

4 Meanwhile, cook the potatoes and carrots in a saucepan of boiling water for 10 minutes. Drain thoroughly and mash them together.

5 Stir the butter, milk and the remaining parsley into the potato and carrot mixture and season with salt and pepper to taste. Spoon the potato on top of the beef mixture to cover it completely; alternatively, pipe the potato over the top with a piping bag.

6 Cook the carrot-topped beef pie in a preheated oven, 190°C/ 375°F/Gas Mark 5, for 45 minutes, or until cooked through. Serve piping hot.

potato, beef & leek pasties

serves four

butter, for greasing

225 g/8 oz waxy potatoes, diced

1 small carrot, diced

225 g/8 oz beef steak, diced

1 leek, sliced

225 g/8 oz ready-made shortcrust
  pastry, thawed if frozen

1 tbsp butter

1 egg beaten

salt and pepper

crisp salad or onion gravy,
  to serve

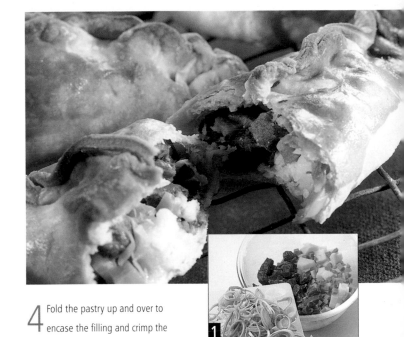

1 Lightly grease a baking tray. Mix the diced potatoes, carrots, beef and sliced leek in a large bowl. Season well with salt and pepper.

2 Divide the pastry into 4 equal portions. On a lightly floured surface, roll out each portion into a 20-cm/8-inch round.

3 Spoon the potato mixture on to the centre of each pastry round. Top the potato mixture with the butter, dividing it equally among the rounds. Brush the pastry edge with a little of the beaten egg.

4 Fold the pastry up and over to encase the filling and crimp the edges together.

5 Transfer the pasties to the prepared baking tray and brush them with the beaten egg.

6 Cook the pasties in a preheated oven, 200°C/400°F/Gas Mark 6, for 20 minutes. Reduce the oven temperature to 160°C/325°F/Gas Mark 3 and cook for 30 minutes.

7 Serve the pasties with a crisp salad or onion gravy.

shepherd's pie

serves four-five

700 g/1 lb 9 oz fresh lean lamb or
  beef mince

2 onions, chopped

225 g/8 oz carrots, diced

1–2 garlic cloves, crushed

1 tbsp plain flour

200 ml/7 fl oz beef stock

200 g/7 oz canned
  chopped tomatoes

1 tsp Worcestershire sauce

1 tsp chopped fresh sage or
  oregano or ½ tsp dried sage
  or oregano

675–900g/1½–2 lb potatoes

2 tbsp butter or margarine

3–4 tbsp skimmed milk

125 g/4½ oz button mushrooms,
  sliced (optional)

salt and pepper

VARIATION

If you like, a mixture of boiled
potatoes and parsnips or swede
may be used for the topping.

---

1 Place the meat in a heavy-based
  saucepan with no extra fat and
cook gently, stirring frequently, until
the meat begins to brown.

2 Add the onions, carrots and garlic
  and continue to cook gently for
about 10 minutes. Stir in the flour and
cook for 2–3 minutes, then gradually
stir in the stock and tomatoes and
bring to the boil.

3 Add the Worcestershire sauce,
  herbs and seasoning, cover the
pan and simmer gently, stirring
occasionally, for about 25 minutes.

4 Cook the potatoes in lightly
  salted, boiling water until tender,
then drain thoroughly and mash,
beating in the butter or margarine,
seasoning and sufficient milk to give a
piping consistency. Place in a piping
bag fitted with a large star nozzle.

5 Stir the mushrooms, if using,
  into the meat and adjust the
seasoning. Turn into a shallow
ovenproof dish.

6 Pipe the potatoes evenly over the
  meat. Cook in a preheated oven,
at 200°C/400°F/Gas Mark 6, for about
30 minutes, until piping hot and the
potatoes are golden brown. Serve.

lamb & potato moussaka

serves four

1 large aubergine, sliced

1 tbsp olive or vegetable oil

1 onion, chopped finely

1 garlic clove, crushed

350 g/12 oz fresh lean lamb mince

250 g/9 oz mushrooms, sliced

425 g/15 oz canned chopped
   tomatoes with herbs

150 ml/5 fl oz lamb or
   vegetable stock

2 tbsp cornflour

2 tbsp water

500 g/1 lb 2 oz potatoes, parboiled
   for 10 minutes and sliced

2 eggs

125 g/4½ oz low-fat
   soft cheese

150 ml/5 fl oz low-fat
   natural yogurt

55 g/2 oz grated low-fat mature
   Cheddar cheese

salt and pepper

fresh flat-leaved parsley,
   to garnish

green salad, to serve

1 Lay the aubergine slices on a clean surface and sprinkle liberally with salt, to extract the bitter juices. Leave for 10 minutes then turn the slices over and repeat. Put in a colander, rinse and drain well.

2 Meanwhile, heat the oil in a saucepan and fry the onion and garlic for 3–4 minutes. Add the lamb and mushrooms and cook for about 5 minutes, until browned. Stir in the tomatoes and stock, bring to the boil and simmer for 10 minutes. Mix the cornflour with the water to a smooth paste and stir into the pan. Cook, stirring, until thickened.

3 Spoon half the mixture into an ovenproof dish. Cover with the aubergine slices, then the remaining lamb mixture. Arrange the sliced potatoes on top.

4 Beat together the eggs, soft cheese and yogurt and season to taste with salt and pepper. Pour over the potatoes to cover them completely. Sprinkle with the grated cheese.

5 Bake in a preheated oven, 190°C/375°F/Gas Mark 5, for 45 minutes, until the topping is set and golden brown. Garnish with flat-leaved parsley and serve with a green salad.

curried stir-fry lamb

serves four

450 g/1 lb potatoes, diced

450 g/1 lb lean lamb, diced

2 tbsp medium-hot curry paste

3 tbsp sunflower oil

1 onion, sliced

1 aubergine, diced

2 garlic cloves, crushed

1 tbsp grated fresh root ginger

150 ml/5 fl oz lamb or beef stock

salt

2 tbsp chopped fresh coriander,
   to garnish

COOK'S TIP

The wok is an ancient Chinese
invention, the name coming from
the Cantonese, meaning a
'cooking vessel'.

VARIATION

Substitute diced skinless,
boneless chicken breast portions
for the lamb and use chicken
stock instead of lamb or beef.

1 Bring a large saucepan of lightly salted water to the boil. Add the potatoes and cook for 10 minutes. Remove the potatoes from the saucepan with a slotted spoon and drain thoroughly.

2 Meanwhile, place the lamb in a large mixing bowl. Add the curry paste and mix well until the lamb is evenly coated in the paste.

3 Heat the sunflower oil in a large preheated wok.

4 Add the onion, aubergine, garlic and ginger to the wok and stir-fry for about 5 minutes.

5 Add the lamb to the wok and stir-fry for a further 5 minutes.

6 Add the lamb or beef stock and cooked potatoes to the wok, bring to the boil and simmer for 30 minutes, or until the lamb is tender and cooked through.

7 Transfer the stir-fry to warm serving dishes and scatter with chopped fresh coriander to garnish. Serve immediately.

lamb & potato masala

serves four

750 g/1 lb 10 oz lean lamb (from
    the leg)

3 tbsp ghee or vegetable oil

500 g/1 lb 2 oz potatoes, peeled
    and cut into large 2.5-cm/
    1-inch pieces

1 large onion, quartered
    and sliced

2 garlic cloves, peeled
    and crushed

175 g/6 oz mushrooms,
    sliced thickly

280 g/10 oz ready-made Tikka
    Masala Curry Sauce

300 ml/10 fl oz water

3 tomatoes, halved and
    sliced thinly

125g/4½ oz spinach, washed and
    stalks trimmed

salt

fresh mint sprigs, to garnish

1 Cut the lamb into 2-cm/1-inch cubes. Heat the ghee or oil in a large pan, add the lamb and fry over a medium heat for 3 minutes, or until sealed all over. Remove the lamb from the pan.

2 Add the potatoes, onion, garlic and mushrooms and fry for 3–4 minutes, stirring frequently.

3 Stir the curry sauce and water into the pan, add the lamb, mix well and season with salt to taste. Cover and cook very gently for 1 hour, or until the lamb is tender and cooked through, stirring occasionally.

4 Add the sliced tomatoes and the spinach to the pan, pushing the leaves well down into the mixture, then cover and cook for a further 10 minutes, until the spinach is cooked and tender.

5 Transfer to warmed serving plates, garnish with mint sprigs and serve hot.

meatballs in spicy sauce

serves four

225 g/8 oz floury potatoes, diced

225 g/8 oz beef or lamb mince

1 onion, chopped finely

1 tbsp chopped fresh coriander

1 celery stick, chopped finely

2 garlic cloves, crushed

2 tbsp butter

1 tbsp vegetable oil

salt and pepper

chopped fresh coriander, to garnish

SAUCE

1 tbsp vegetable oil

1 onion, chopped finely

2 tsp soft brown sugar

400 g/14 oz canned
   chopped tomatoes

1 fresh green chilli, deseeded
   and chopped

1 tsp paprika

150 ml/5 fl oz vegetable stock

2 tsp cornflour

1 Cook the diced potatoes in a saucepan of boiling water for 25 minutes, until cooked through. Drain well and transfer to a large mixing bowl. Mash until smooth.

2 Add the beef or lamb mince, onion, coriander, celery, garlic and seasoning and mix together well.

3 Bring the mixture together with your hands and roll it into 20 small balls.

4 To make the sauce, heat the oil in a pan and sauté the onion for 5 minutes. Add the remaining sauce ingredients and bring to the boil, stirring constantly. Lower the heat and simmer for 20 minutes.

5 Meanwhile, heat the butter and oil for the meatballs in a frying pan. Add the meatballs, in batches, and cook, turning frequently, for

10–15 minutes, until browned. Keep warm while cooking the remainder. Transfer the meatballs to a warm, shallow dish and serve with the sauce poured around them and garnished with the fresh coriander.

spanish potato bake

serves four

675 g/1½ lb waxy potatoes, diced

3 tbsp olive oil

1 onion, halved and sliced

2 garlic cloves, crushed

400 g/14 oz canned plum
   tomatoes, chopped

75 g/2¾ oz chorizo sausage, sliced

1 green pepper, deseeded and cut
   into strips

½ tsp paprika

25 g/1 oz stoned black
   olives, halved

8 eggs

1 tbsp chopped fresh parsley

salt and pepper

crusty bread, to serve

VARIATION

Add a little spice to the dish by
incorporating 1 teaspoon chilli
powder in step 4, if desired.

---

1 Cook the diced potatoes in a saucepan of boiling water for 10 minutes, or until softened. Drain and reserve.

2 Heat the olive oil in a large frying pan, add the onion and garlic and fry gently for 2–3 minutes, until the onion has softened.

3 Add the tomatoes and cook over a low heat, stirring occasionally, for about 10 minutes, until the mixture has reduced slightly.

4 Stir the potatoes into the pan with the chorizo, green pepper, paprika and olives. Season to taste with salt and pepper. Cook, stirring constantly, for 5 minutes. Transfer to a shallow ovenproof dish.

5 Make 8 small hollows in the top of the mixture with the back of a spoon and carefully break an egg into each hollow. Season the eggs with salt and pepper.

6 Cook in a preheated oven, 220°C/425°F/Gas Mark 7, for 5–6 minutes, or until the eggs are just cooked and set.

7 Sprinkle with chopped parsley and serve immediately with plenty of crusty bread.

potato, sausage & onion pie

serves four

2 large waxy potatoes, unpeeled
   and sliced

2 tbsp butter

4 thick pork and herb sausages

1 leek, sliced

2 garlic cloves, crushed

150 ml/5 fl oz vegetable stock

150 ml/5 fl oz dry cider or
   apple juice

2 tbsp chopped fresh sage

2 tbsp cornflour

4 tbsp water

75 g/2¾ oz mature cheese, grated

salt and pepper

1 Cook the sliced potatoes in a saucepan of boiling water for 10 minutes. Drain and reserve.

2 Meanwhile, melt the butter in a frying pan and cook the sausages for 8–10 minutes, turning them frequently so that they brown on all sides. Remove the sausages from the pan and cut them into thick slices.

3 Add the leek, garlic and sausage slices to the pan and cook for 2–3 minutes.

4 Add the vegetable stock, cider or apple juice and sage. Season with salt and pepper to taste.

5 Blend the cornflour with the water. Stir it into the pan and bring to the boil, stirring until the sauce is thick and clear. Spoon the mixture into the base of a deep pie dish.

6 Layer the potato slices on top. Season to taste with salt and pepper and sprinkle the grated cheese over the top.

7 Cook in a preheated oven, 190°C/375°F/Gas Mark 5, for 25–30 minutes, or until the potatoes are cooked and the cheese is golden brown. Serve hot.

tomato & sausage pan-fry

serves four

600 g/1 lb 5 oz potatoes, sliced

1 tbsp vegetable oil

8 flavoured sausages

1 red onion, cut into 8 wedges

1 tbsp tomato purée

150 ml/5 fl oz red wine

150 ml/5 fl oz passata

2 large tomatoes, each cut into
    8 pieces

175 g/6 oz broccoli
    florets, blanched

2 tbsp chopped fresh basil

salt and pepper

shredded fresh basil, to garnish

1 Cook the sliced potatoes in a large saucepan of boiling water for 7 minutes. Drain the potatoes thoroughly and reserve.

2 Meanwhile, heat the oil in a large frying pan. Add the sausages and cook for 5 minutes, turning the sausages frequently to ensure that they are browned on all sides.

3 Add the onion wedges to the pan and continue to cook for a further 5 minutes, stirring frequently.

4 Stir in the tomato purée, red wine and the passata and mix together well. Add the tomato wedges, broccoli florets and chopped basil to the pan-fry and mix together carefully.

5 Add the parboiled potato slices to the pan. Cook for about 10 minutes, or until the sausages are completely cooked through. Season to taste with salt and pepper.

6 Garnish the pan-fry with fresh shredded basil and serve hot.

veal italienne

serves four

5 tbsp butter

1 tbsp olive oil

675 g/1½ lb potatoes, diced

4 veal escalopes, 175 g/6 oz each

1 onion, cut into 8 wedges

2 garlic cloves, crushed

2 tbsp plain flour

2 tbsp tomato purée

150 ml/5 fl oz red wine

300 ml/10 fl oz chicken stock

8 ripe tomatoes, skinned, seeded
    and diced

25 g/1 oz stoned black olives,
    halved

2 tbsp chopped fresh basil

salt and pepper

fresh basil leaves, to garnish

COOK'S TIP

For a quicker cooking time and
really tender meat, pound the
meat with a meat mallet to
flatten it slightly before cooking.

1 Heat the butter and oil in a large, heavy-based frying pan. Add the diced potatoes and cook for 5–7 minutes, stirring frequently, until they begin to brown.

2 Remove the potatoes from the pan with a slotted spoon and drain on kitchen paper..

3 Place the veal in the frying pan and cook for 2–3 minutes on each side, until sealed. Remove from the pan and reserve.

4 Stir the onion and garlic into the pan and cook for 2–3 minutes.

5 Add the flour and tomato purée and cook for 1 minute, stirring. Gradually blend in the red wine and chicken stock, stirring to make a smooth sauce.

6 Return the potatoes and veal to the pan. Stir in the tomatoes, olives and basil and season to taste with salt and pepper.

7 Transfer to a casserole and cook in a preheated oven, 180°C/350°F/Gas Mark 4, for 1 hour, or until the potatoes and veal are cooked through. Garnish with basil leaves and serve immediately.

potato & broccoli pie

serves four

450 g/1 lb waxy potatoes, cut
    into chunks

2 tbsp butter

1 tbsp vegetable oil

175 g/6 oz lean pork, diced

1 red onion, cut into 8 wedges

2½ tbsp plain flour, plus extra
    for dusting

150 ml/5 fl oz vegetable stock

150 ml/5 fl oz milk

75 g/2¾ oz dolcelatte
    cheese, crumbled

175 g/6 oz broccoli florets

25 g/1 oz walnuts

225 g/8 oz ready-made puff pastry,
    thawed if frozen

milk, for glazing

salt and pepper

COOK'S TIP

Use a semi-hard cheese, such as
mature Cheddar, instead of the
dolcelatte, if you prefer.

1 Cook the potato chunks in a saucepan of boiling water for 5 minutes. Drain and reserve.

2 Meanwhile, heat the butter and oil in a heavy-based pan. Add the pork and cook for 5 minutes, turning until browned.

3 Add the onion and cook for a further 2 minutes. Stir in the flour and cook for 1 minute, then gradually stir in the vegetable stock and milk. Bring to the boil, stirring constantly.

4 Add the cheese, broccoli florets, potatoes and walnuts to the pan and simmer for 5 minutes. Season with salt and pepper, then spoon the mixture into a pie dish.

5 On a floured surface, roll out the pastry until 2.5-cm/1-inch larger than the dish. Cut a 2.5-cm/1-inch wide strip from the pastry. Dampen the edge of the dish and place the pastry strip around it. Brush with milk and put the pastry lid on top.

6 Seal and crimp the edges and make 2 small slits in the centre of the lid. Brush with milk and then cook in a preheated oven, 200°C/400°F/Gas Mark 6, for 25 minutes, or until the pastry has risen and is golden.

strained dhal with meatballs

serves six

200 g/7 oz masoor dhal (lentils)

850 ml/1½ pints water

1 tsp crushed fresh root ginger

1 tsp crushed fresh garlic

½ tsp ground turmeric

1½ tsp chilli powder

1½ tsp salt

3 tbsp lemon juice

450 g/1 lb canned meatballs

TO GARNISH

3 fresh green chillies, deseeded and
    chopped finely

fresh coriander leaves, chopped

BAGHAAR

150 ml/5 fl oz vegetable oil

3 garlic cloves

4 dried red chillies

1 tsp white cumin seeds

FRIED POTATOES

pinch of salt

2 medium potatoes, sliced thinly

300 ml/10 fl oz vegetable oil

1 Rinse the lentils, and pick through them to remove any stones.

2 Place the lentils in a saucepan and cover with 600 ml/1 pint of the water. Add the ginger, garlic, turmeric and chilli powder and bring to the boil and cook until the lentils are soft and mushy. Add the salt, stirring.

3 Mash the lentils, then push them through a sieve, reserving the liquid. Add the lemon juice to the strained liquid.

4 Stir the rest of the water into the strained liquid and bring to the boil over a low heat. Drop the meatballs gently into the lentil mixture, and keep warm.

5 Prepare the baghaar. Heat the oil in a pan. Add the garlic, dried red chillies and white cumin seeds and fry for 2 minutes. Pour the baghaar over the lentil mixture, stirring to mix.

6 For the fried potato, rub the salt over the potato slices. Heat the oil in a frying pan and fry the potatoes, turning, until crisp. Garnish the meatballs with the fried potatoes, chillies and coriander.

quick chicken bake

serves four

500 g/1 lb 2 oz fresh chicken mince

1 large onion, chopped finely

2 carrots, chopped finely

2 tbsp plain flour

1 tbsp tomato purée

300 ml/10 fl oz chicken stock

pinch of fresh thyme

1.5 kg/3 lb 5 oz mashed potatoes,
   creamed with butter and milk
   and well seasoned

75 g/2¾ oz grated cheese, such
   as Cheddar

salt and pepper

cooked peas, to serve

1 Brown the chicken mince, onion and carrots in a non-stick frying pan over a medium heat, stirring frequently, for 5 minutes.

2 Sprinkle the chicken with the flour and simmer for a further 2 minutes.

3 Gradually blend in the tomato purée and stock, then simmer for 15 minutes. Season and add the fresh thyme.

4 Transfer the chicken and vegetable mixture to a casserole and leave to cool.

5 Spoon the mashed potato over the chicken mixture and sprinkle with cheese. Bake in a preheated oven, 200°C/400°F/Gas Mark 6, for about 20 minutes, or until the cheese is bubbling and golden. Serve, straight from the casserole, with the peas.

potato crisp pie

serves four

600 g/1 lb 5 oz waxy
 potatoes, sliced

5 tbsp butter

1 skinned chicken breast fillet, about
 175 g/6 oz

2 garlic cloves, crushed

4 spring onions, sliced

2½ tbsp plain flour

150 ml/5 fl oz dry white wine

150 ml/5 fl oz double cream

225 g/8 oz broccoli florets

4 large tomatoes, sliced

85 g/3 oz Gruyère cheese, sliced

225 ml/8 fl oz natural yogurt

25 g/1 oz rolled oats, toasted

1 Cook the potatoes in a saucepan of boiling water for 10 minutes. Drain and reserve.

2 Meanwhile, melt the butter in a frying pan. Cut the chicken into strips and cook for 5 minutes, turning. Add the garlic and spring onions and cook for a further 2 minutes.

3 Stir in the flour and cook for 1 minute. Gradually add the wine and cream. Bring to the boil, stirring, then reduce the heat until the sauce is simmering, then cook for 5 minutes.

4 Meanwhile, blanch the broccoli in boiling water, drain and refresh in cold water.

5 Place half of the potatoes in the base of a pie dish and top with half of the tomatoes and half of the broccoli florets.

6 Spoon the chicken sauce on top and repeat the layers in the same order once more.

7 Arrange the Gruyère cheese on top and spoon over the yogurt. Sprinkle with the oats and cook in a preheated oven, 200°C/400°F/Gas Mark 6, for 25 minutes, until the top is golden brown. Serve the potato crisp pie immediately.

gardener's chicken

serves four

250 g/9 oz parsnips, peeled
  and chopped

2 small carrots, peeled and chopped

25 g/1 oz fresh breadcrumbs

¼ tsp freshly grated nutmeg

1 tbsp chopped fresh parsley, plus
  extra to garnish

1.5 kg/3 lb 5 oz chicken

bunch of fresh parsley

½ onion, cut into wedges

2 tbsp butter, softened

4 tbsp olive oil

500 g/1 lb 2 oz new
  potatoes, scrubbed

500 g/1 lb 2 oz baby carrots,
  washed and trimmed

salt and pepper

COOK'S TIP

The quickest way to make 25 g/
1 oz fresh breadcrumbs is to cut
the crusts off 1 thick or 2 thin
sliced of bread and process in a
food processor for a few
seconds. This produces more
even-size crumbs than grating
and spares the knuckles.

1 To make the stuffing, put the parsnips and carrots into a pan, cover with water and bring to the boil. Cover the pan and simmer until tender. Drain well, then process in a blender or food processor. Transfer the purée to a bowl and leave to cool.

2 Mix in the breadcrumbs, nutmeg and chopped parsley and season to taste with salt and pepper.

3 Put the stuffing into the neck end of the chicken and push a little under the skin over the breast meat. Secure the flap of skin with a small metal skewer or cocktail stick.

4 Place the bunch of parsley and onion inside the cavity of the chicken, then place the chicken in a large roasting tin.

5 Spread the butter over the skin and season with salt and pepper, cover with foil and place in a preheated oven, 190°C/375°F/Gas Mark 5, for 30 minutes.

6 Meanwhile, heat the oil in a frying pan, and lightly brown the potatoes.

7 Transfer the potatoes to the roasting tin and add the baby carrots. Baste the chicken and continue to cook for a further hour, basting the chicken and vegetables after 30 minutes. Remove the foil for the last 20 minutes to allow the skin to crisp. Garnish the vegetables with chopped parsley and serve.

chicken & potato casserole

serves four

2 tbsp vegetable oil

5 tbsp butter

4 chicken portions, about 225 g/
     8 oz each

2 leeks, sliced

1 garlic clove, crushed

4 tbsp plain flour

850 ml/1½ pints chicken stock

300 ml/10 fl oz dry white wine

125 g/4½ oz baby carrots,
     halved lengthways

125 g/4½ oz baby sweetcorn cobs,
     halved lengthways

450 g/1 lb small new potatoes

bouquet garni

150 ml/5 fl oz double cream

salt and pepper

rice or broccoli, to serve

1 Heat the oil and butter in a large frying pan. Cook the chicken for 10 minutes, turning until browned all over. Transfer the chicken to a casserole using a slotted spoon.

2 Add the leeks and garlic to the pan and cook for 2–3 minutes, stirring constantly. Stir in the flour and cook for 1 further minute. Remove the frying pan from the heat and stir in the stock and wine. Season well.

3 Return the pan to the heat and bring the mixture to the boil. Stir in the carrots, sweetcorn, new potatoes and bouquet garni.

4 Transfer the mixture to the casserole. Cover and cook in a preheated oven, 180°C/350°F/Gas Mark 4, for about 1 hour.

5 Remove the casserole from the oven and stir in the cream. Return the casserole to the oven, uncovered, and cook for a further 15 minutes. Remove the bouquet garni and discard. Taste and adjust the seasoning, if necessary. Serve the casserole with plain rice or fresh vegetables, such as broccoli.

chicken & banana cakes

serves four

450 g/1 lb floury potatoes, diced

225 g/8 oz fresh chicken mince

1 large banana

2 tbsp plain flour

1 tsp lemon juice

1 onion, chopped finely

2 tbsp chopped fresh sage

2 tbsp butter

2 tbsp vegetable oil

150 ml/5 fl oz single cream

150 ml/5 fl oz chicken stock

salt and pepper

fresh sage leaves, to garnish

1 Cook the diced potatoes in a saucepan of boiling water for 10 minutes, until cooked through. Drain and mash the potatoes until smooth. Stir in the minced chicken.

2 Mash the banana with a fork and add it to the potato with the flour, lemon juice, onion and half of the chopped sage. Season well and stir the mixture together.

3 Divide the mixture into 8 equal portions. With lightly floured hands, gently shape each portion into a round patty.

4 Heat the butter and oil in a frying pan, add the potato cakes and cook for 12–15 minutes, or until cooked through, turning once. Remove from the pan and keep warm.

5 Stir in the cream and stock with the remaining chopped sage. Cook over a low heat for 2–3 minutes.

6 Arrange the potato cakes on a serving plate, garnish with fresh sage leaves and serve with the cream and sage sauce.

potato, leek & chicken pie

serves four

225 g/8 oz waxy potatoes, diced

5 tbsp butter

1 skinned chicken breast fillet, about
175 g/6 oz, diced

1 leek, sliced

150 g/5½ oz chestnut
mushrooms, sliced

2½ tbsp plain flour

300 ml/10 fl oz milk

1 tbsp Dijon mustard

2 tbsp chopped fresh sage

225 g/8 oz filo pastry, thawed
if frozen

3 tbsp butter, melted

salt and pepper

1 Cook the diced potatoes in a
saucepan of boiling water for
5 minutes. Drain and reserve.

2 Melt the butter in a frying pan
and cook the diced chicken for
5 minutes, or until browned all over.

3 Add the leek and mushrooms
and cook over a medium heat,
stirring frequently, for 3 minutes. Stir in
the flour and cook for 1 minute, stirring
constantly. Gradually add the milk and
bring to the boil. Add the mustard,
sage and potatoes, then simmer for 10
minutes.

4 Meanwhile, line a deep pie dish
with half of the sheets of filo
pastry. Spoon the sauce into the dish
and cover with one sheet of pastry.
Brush the pastry with butter and lay
another sheet on top. Brush this sheet
with butter.

5 Cut the remaining filo pastry
into strips and fold them on to
the top of the pie to create a ruffled
effect. Brush the strips with the melted
butter and cook in a preheated oven,
180°C/350°F/Gas Mark 4, for about
45 minutes. or until golden brown and
crisp. Serve hot.

COOK'S TIP

If the top of the pie starts
to brown too quickly, cover it
with foil halfway through the
cooking time to allow the pastry
base to cook through without
the top burning.

chicken & potato bake

serves four

2 tbsp olive oil

4 lean chicken breasts

bunch of spring onions, trimmed
and chopped

350 g/12 oz young spring carrots,
scrubbed and sliced

125 g/4½ oz French green beans,
trimmed and sliced

600 ml/1 pint chicken stock

350 g/12 oz small new
potatoes, scrubbed

1 small bunch of mixed fresh herbs,
such as thyme, rosemary, bay
and parsley

2 tbsp cornflour

2–3 tbsp cold water

salt and pepper

fresh mixed herb sprigs,
to garnish

2 Add the spring onions, carrots
and green beans and gently fry
for 3–4 minutes.

3 Return the chicken to the
casserole and pour in the stock.
Add the potatoes and herbs. Season,
bring to the boil, then cover the
casserole and transfer to the oven.
Bake in a preheated oven, 190°C/
375°F/Gas Mark 5, for 40–50 minutes,
until the potatoes are tender.

1 Heat the oil in a large flameproof
casserole and add the chicken
breasts. Gently fry for 5–8 minutes,
until browned on both sides. Remove
from the casserole with a slotted spoon
and reserve.

4 Blend the cornflour with the cold
water to a smooth paste. Add to
the casserole, stirring until blended and
thickened. Cover and cook for a further
5 minutes. Garnish with fresh herbs
and serve immediately.

potato & turkey pie

serves four

300 g/10½ oz waxy potatoes, diced

2 tbsp butter

1 tbsp vegetable oil

300 g/10½ oz fresh turkey
    meat, diced

1 red onion, halved and sliced

2 tbsp plain flour, plus extra
    for dusting

300 ml/10 fl oz milk

150 ml/5 fl oz double cream

2 celery sticks, sliced

75 g/2¾ oz dried apricots, chopped

25 g/1 oz walnut pieces

2 tbsp chopped fresh parsley

225 g/8 oz ready-made
    shortcrust pastry

beaten egg, for brushing

salt and pepper

1 Cook the diced potatoes in a
large saucepan of boiling water
for about 10 minutes, until tender.
Drain and reserve.

2 Meanwhile, heat the butter with
the vegetable oil in a large,
heavy-based saucepan. Add the turkey
and cook over a medium heat, stirring,
for 5 minutes, until browned.

3 Add the sliced onion and cook for
2–3 minutes. Stir in the flour and
cook for 1 minute. Gradually stir in the
milk and the double cream. Bring to
the boil, stirring, then reduce the heat
until the mixture is simmering.

4 Stir in the celery, apricots, walnut
pieces, parsley and potatoes.
Season well. Spoon the mixture into the
base of a 1.2-litres/2-pint pie dish.

5 On a lightly floured surface, roll
out the pastry until it is 1-inch/
2.5-cm larger than the dish. Trim a
1-inch/2.5-cm wide strip from the
pastry and place on the dampened rim
of the dish. Brush with water and cover
with the pastry lid, pressing to seal.

6 Brush the top of the pie with
beaten egg and cook in a
preheated oven, 200°C/400°F/Gas
Mark 6, for 25–30 minutes, or until the
pastry is cooked and golden brown.
Serve at once.

Fish

There is no denying that fish and potatoes are a terrific combination. In these recipes, potatoes are used in a variety of ways to enhance the fish. They are used to form a crispy coating for cod, and mashed to make the basis of fish cakes and fritters. They are sliced to form part of a layered pie, and sautéed with shallots to create the perfect accompaniment to a red mullet wrapped in Parma ham. For health-conscious cooks, the nutritious value of these dishes is unbeatable.

salt cod fritters

serves six

450 g/1 lb salt cod

350 g/12 oz floury baking potatoes

1 tbsp olive oil, plus extra for
    deep frying

1 onion, very finely chopped

1 garlic clove, crushed

4 tbsp very finely chopped fresh
    parsley or coriander

1 tbsp capers in brine, drained and
    chopped finely, (optional)

1 small egg, lightly beaten

salt and pepper

fresh parsley, to garnish

aïoli, to serve

1 Break the salt cod into pieces and place in a bowl. Add enough water to cover and leave for 48 hours, changing the water 4 times.

2 Drain the salt cod, then cook in boiling water for 20–25 minutes, until tender. Drain, then remove all the skin and bones. Using a fork, flake the fish into fine pieces that still retain some texture.

3 Meanwhile, boil the potatoes in their skins until tender. Drain, peel and mash in a large bowl. Set aside.

4 Heat the 1 tablespoon of the oil in a frying pan. Add the onion and garlic and fry for 5 minutes, stirring, until tender but not brown. Remove with a slotted spoon and drain on kitchen paper.

5 Stir the salt cod, onion and garlic into the mashed potatoes. Stir in the parsley and capers, if using. Season generously with pepper.

6 Stir in the beaten egg. Cover and chill for 30 minutes, then adjust the seasoning.

7 Heat 5-cm/2-inch of oil in a deep fryer to 180–190°C/350–375°F, or until a cube of bread browns in 30 seconds. Drop tablespoonfuls of the salt-cod mixture into the hot oil and fry for about 8 minutes, or until golden brown and set. Do not fry more than 6 at a time because the oil will become too cold and the fritters will become soggy. You will get 18–20 fritters.

8 Drain the fritters on kitchen paper. Serve at once with aïoli for dipping. Garnish with parsley.

tuna & cheese quiche

serves four

450 g/1 lb floury potatoes, diced

2 tbsp butter

6 tbsp plain flour, plus extra
    for dusting

mixed vegetables or salad, to serve

FILLING

1 tbsp vegetable oil

1 shallot, chopped

1 garlic clove, crushed

1 red pepper, deseeded and diced

175g/6 oz drained canned tuna
    in brine

50 g/1¾ oz drained
    canned sweetcorn

150 ml/5 fl oz skimmed milk

3 eggs, beaten

1 tbsp chopped fresh dill

50 g/1¾ oz mature low-fat
    cheese, grated

salt and pepper

mixed vegetables or salad, to serve

TO GARNISH

fresh dill sprigs

lemon wedges

1 Cook the potatoes in a large pan of boiling water for 10 minutes, or until tender.

2 Drain and mash with a fork or potato masher. Add the butter and flour and mix to form a dough.

3 Knead the potato dough on a floured surface and press into a 20-cm/8-inch flan tin. Prick the base with a fork. Line with baking paper and baking beans and bake blind in a preheated oven, 200°C/400°F/Gas Mark 6, for 20 minutes.

4 Heat the oil in a frying pan and gently cook the shallot, garlic and red pepper for 5 minutes. Spoon into the flan case. Flake the tuna and arrange in the flan with the sweetcorn.

5 In a bowl, mix the milk, eggs and chopped dill and season.

6 Pour the egg and dill mixture into the flan case and sprinkle the grated cheese on top.

7 Bake in the oven for 20 minutes. or until the filling has set. Garnish the quiche with fresh dill and lemon wedges. Serve with mixed vegetables or salad.

cod & chips

serves four

675 g/1 lb 8 oz potatoes

4 pieces cod fillet

oil for deep frying

BATTER

15 g/½ oz fresh yeast

300 ml/ 10 fl oz beer

225 g/8 oz plain flour

½-1 tsp salt

MAYONNAISE

1 egg yolk

1 tsp wholegrain mustard

1 tbsp lemon juice

200 ml/7 fl oz light olive oil

salt and pepper

fresh parsley sprigs

1 For the batter, cream the yeast with a little of the beer to a smooth paste. Gradually stir in the remaining beer. Sift the plain flour and salt into a bowl, make a well in the centre and add the yeast mixture. Gradually whisk to a smooth batter. Cover and leave for 1 hour.

2 For the mayonnaise, put the egg yolk, mustard, lemon juice and seasoning into a food processor. Blend for 30 seconds. Begin adding the olive oil, drop by drop, until the mixture begins to thicken. Continue adding the oil in a slow, steady stream until all the oil has been incorporated. Taste for seasoning. Thin with a little hot water if the mayonnaise is too thick, chill.

3 For the fish and chips, cut the potatoes into chips about 1.5-cm/ ½-inch thick. Heat a deep-fat fryer half filled with vegetable oil to140°C/275°F or until a cube of bread browns in 1 minute. Cook the chips in 2 batches for about 5 minutes, until they are soft but not browned. Place the chips to drain on kitchen paper and reserve.

4 Increase the heat to 160°C/ 325°F or until a cube of bread browns in 45 seconds. Season the fish then dip into the batter. Fry 2 pieces at a time for 7–8 minutes, until deep golden brown and cooked through. Drain well on kitchen paper and keep warm while you cook remaining fish. Keep these warm while you finish cooking the chips.

5 Increase the heat to 190°C/ 375°F or until a cube of bread browns in 30 seconds. Fry the chips again, in 2 batches, for 2–3 minutes, until crisp and golden. Drain on kitchen paper and sprinkle with salt.

6 Serve the fish with the chips and mayonnaise. Serve while still hot, garnished with lemon wedges and parsley sprigs.

203

soused trout & potato salad

serves four

4 trout, about 225–350 g/8–12 oz
   each, filleted

1 onion, very thinly sliced

2 bay leaves

fresh parsley and dill sprigs, or other
   fresh herbs

10–12 black peppercorns

4–6 cloves

good pinch of salt

150 ml/5 fl oz red wine vinegar

salad leaves, to garnish

POTATO SALAD

500 g/1 lb 2 oz small new potatoes

2 tbsp French dressing

4 tbsp low-fat mayonnaise

3–4 spring onions, chopped

salt

1 Trim the trout fillets, cutting off any pieces of fin. If preferred, remove the skin – use a sharp knife and, beginning at the tail end, carefully cut the flesh from the skin, pressing the knife down firmly as you go.

2 Lightly grease a shallow ovenproof dish and lay the fillets in it, packing them fairly tightly together but keeping them in a single layer. Arrange the sliced onion, bay leaves and herbs over the fish.

3 Put the peppercorns, cloves, salt and vinegar into a pan and bring almost to the boil. Remove from the heat and pour evenly over the fish. Leave to cool, then cover and marinate in the refrigerator for 24 hours.

4 Cover the dish with foil and cook in a preheated oven, 160°C/ 325°F/ Gas Mark 3 for 15 minutes. Leave until cold and then cover and chill thoroughly.

5 Cook the potatoes in boiling salted water for 10–15 minutes, until just tender. Drain. While still warm, cut into large dice and place in a bowl. Combine the French dressing and mayonnaise, add to the potatoes while warm and toss evenly. Leave until cold, then sprinkle the potato salad with chopped spring onions.

6 Place the fish on serving plates, pour a little of the juices over each portion of fish. Garnish with salad leaves and serve with the potato salad.

layered fish & potato pie

serves four

900 g/2 lb waxy potatoes, sliced

5 tbsp butter

1 red onion, halved and sliced

5 tbsp plain flour

450 ml/16 fl oz milk

150 ml/5 fl oz double cream

225 g/8 oz smoked haddock
   fillet, skinned and diced

225 g/8 oz cod fillet, skinned and
   diced

1 red pepper, deseeded and diced

125 g/4½ oz broccoli florets

50 g/1¾ oz Parmesan cheese, grated

   salt and pepper

1 Cook the sliced potatoes in a saucepan of boiling water for 10 minutes. Drain and reserve.

2 Meanwhile, melt the butter in a saucepan, add the onion and fry gently for 3–4 minutes.

3 Add the flour and cook for 1 minute. Blend in the milk and cream and bring to the boil, stirring until the sauce has thickened.

4 Arrange about half of the potato slices in the base of a shallow, ovenproof dish.

5 Add the fish, red pepper and broccoli to the sauce and cook over a low heat for 10 minutes. Season with salt and pepper, then spoon the mixture over the potatoes in the dish.

6 Arrange the remaining potato slices in a layer over the fish mixture. Sprinkle the Parmesan cheese over the top.

7 Cook in a preheated oven, 180°C/ 350°F/Gas Mark 4, for about 30 minutes, until the top is golden.

fish balls with tomato sauce

serves four

450 g/1 lb floury potatoes, diced

3 tbsp butter

225 g/8 oz smoked fish fillet, such
   as cod, skinned

2 eggs, beaten

1 tbsp chopped fresh dill

½ tsp cayenne pepper

vegetable oil for deep-frying

salt and pepper

SAUCE

300 ml/10 fl oz passata

1 tbsp tomato purée

2 tbsp chopped fresh dill

150 ml/5 fl oz fish stock

1 Cook the diced potatoes in a saucepan of boiling water for 10 minutes, or until tender. Drain well, then add the butter to the potato and mash until smooth. Season well with salt and pepper.

2 Meanwhile, poach the fish in boiling water for 10 minutes, turning once. Drain and mash the fish. Stir it into the potato mixture and leave to cool.

3 While the potato and fish mixture is cooling, make the sauce. Put the passata, tomato purée, dill and stock in a pan and bring to the boil. Reduce the heat, cover the pan and simmer for 20 minutes, until thickened.

4 Add the eggs, dill and cayenne pepper to the potato and fish mixture and beat until well mixed.

5 In a large saucepan or deep-fat fryer, heat the oil to 180–190°C/ 350–375°F or until a cube of bread browns in 30 seconds. Drop dessertspoons of the potato mixture into the oil and cook for 3–4 minutes, until golden brown. Drain well on kitchen paper.

6 Garnish the potato and fish balls with fresh dill sprigs, if liked, and serve with the tomato sauce.

207

smoked fish pie

1 For the sauce, heat the butter in a large saucepan and when melted, add the flour and mustard powder. Stir until smooth and cook over a very low heat for 2 minutes without colouring. Gradually whisk in the milk until smooth. Simmer gently for 2 minutes, then stir in the grated cheese until smooth. Remove the pan from the heat and put some clingfilm over the surface of the sauce to prevent a skin from forming. Reserve.

2 Meanwhile, for the topping, cook the whole potatoes in plenty of salted, boiling water for 15 minutes. Drain well and leave until cool enough to handle.

3 Heat the olive oil in a clean pan and add the onion. Cook for 5 minutes, until softened. Add the sliced leek, the diced carrot and celery and the mushrooms and cook for a further 10 minutes, until the vegetables have softened. Stir in the lemon rind and cook briefly.

4 Add the softened vegetables with the fish, prawns, parsley and dill to the sauce. Season to taste and transfer to a greased 1.75-litre/3-pint casserole.

5 Peel the cooled potatoes and grate them coarsely. Mix with the melted butter. Cover the filling with the grated potato and sprinkle with the grated Gruyère cheese.

6 Cover loosely with foil and bake in a preheated oven, 200°C/ 400° F/Gas Mark 6, for 30 minutes. Remove the foil and bake for an additional 30 minutes, until the topping is tender and golden and the filling is bubbling. Garnish and serve the smoked fish pie immediately with your favourite selection of vegetables.

fish pasties

serves four

PASTRY

450 g/1 lb self-raising flour, plus
    extra for dusting

pinch of salt

225 g/8 oz butter, diced, plus extra
    for greasing

1 egg, lightly beaten

FILLING

4 tbsp butter

1 small leek, diced

1 small onion, chopped finely

1 carrot, diced

225 g/8 oz potatoes, diced

350 g/12 oz firm white fish fillet, cut
    into 2.5-cm/1-inch pieces

4 tsp white wine vinegar

25 g/1 oz Cheddar cheese, grated

1 tsp chopped fresh tarragon

salt and pepper

TO GARNISH

mixed salad leaves

cherry tomatoes

1 In a large bowl, sift together the flour and salt. Add the butter and rub it in with your fingertips until the mixture resembles coarse breadcrumbs. Add about 3 tablespoons cold water and bring together to form a dough. Knead briefly until smooth. Wrap in clingfilm and chill in the refrigerator for 30 minutes.

2 Meanwhile, to make the filling, melt half the butter in a large frying pan and add the leek, onion and carrot. Cook over a low heat, stirring occasionally, for 7–8 minutes, until the vegetables have softened. Remove the pan from the heat, put to one side and leave the mixture to cool slightly.

3 Put the vegetable mixture into a large mixing bowl and add the potatoes, fish, vinegar, remaining butter, cheese, tarragon and seasoning. Cover lightly and reserve.

4 Remove the pastry from the refrigerator and roll out thinly on a lightly floured surface. Using a pastry cutter, press out 4 x 19-cm/7½-inch rounds. Alternatively, use a small plate of a similar size as a template and cut around it with a sharp knife. Divide the filling among the 4 rounds. Moisten the edges of the pastry and fold over. Pinch to seal. Crimp the edges firmly and place the pasties on a lightly greased baking tray. Brush generously with the beaten egg to glaze, avoiding the base of the pastry to prevent the pasties from sticking to the baking tray.

5 Bake the pasties in a preheated oven, 200°C/400°F/Gas Mark 6, for 15 minutes. Remove from the oven and brush again with the egg glaze. Return to the oven for a further 20 minutes or until golden brown and cooked through. Serve hot or cold with the mixed salad and tomatoes.

ocean pie

serves four

500 g/1 lb 2 oz cod or haddock
    fillet, skinned

225 g/8 oz salmon steak

425 ml/15 fl oz skimmed milk

1 bay leaf

1 kg/2 lb 4 oz potatoes

55 g/2 oz peeled prawns, thawed
    if frozen

4 tbsp butter or margarine

4 tbsp plain flour

2–4 tbsp white wine

1 tsp chopped fresh dill or
    ½ tsp dried dill

2 tbsp drained capers

salt and pepper

few whole prawns in their shells,
    to garnish

VARIATION

Substitute fresh scallops for the prawns in the pie. Sear them briefly in hot oil for 1–2 minutes before adding them to the filling in step 3. Cut them in half first if they are large.

1 Put the fish into a saucepan with 300 ml/10 fl oz of the milk, the bay leaf and seasoning. Bring to the boil, cover and simmer gently for 10–15 minutes, until tender.

2 Coarsely chop the potatoes and cook in lightly salted, boiling water until tender.

3 Drain the fish, reserving the cooking liquid. Measure the cooking liquid and make up to 300 ml/10 fl oz with more milk if necessary. Flake the fish, discarding any bones and place in a shallow ovenproof dish. Add the prawns.

4 Melt half the butter or margarine in a saucepan, add the flour and cook, stirring, for 1–2 minutes. Gradually stir in the reserved milk and the wine and bring to the boil. Add the dill, capers and seasoning to taste and simmer until thickened. Pour over the fish and mix well.

5 Drain the potatoes and mash, adding the remaining butter or margarine, seasoning and sufficient milk to give a piping consistency.

6 Put the mashed potato into a piping bag. Use a large star nozzle and pipe over the fish. Cook in a preheated oven at 200°C/400°F/Gas Mark 6, for about 25 minutes, until piping hot and browned. Serve garnished with the whole prawns.

poached rainbow trout

serves four

1.3 kg/3 lb rainbow trout, filleted

700 g/1 lb 9 oz new potatoes

3 spring onions, finely chopped

1 egg, hard-boiled and chopped

salad leaves to serve

COURT-BOUILLON

850 ml/1½ pints cold water

850 ml/1½ pints dry white wine

3 tbsp white wine vinegar

2 large carrots, chopped roughly

1 onion, chopped roughly

2 celery sticks, chopped roughly

2 leeks, chopped roughly

2 garlic cloves, chopped roughly

2 fresh bay leaves

4 fresh parsley sprigs

4 fresh thyme sprigs

6 black peppercorns

1 tsp salt

WATERCRESS MAYONNAISE

1 egg yolk

1 tsp Dijon mustard

1 tsp white wine vinegar

55 g/2 oz watercress

   leaves, chopped

225 ml/8 fl oz light olive oil

salt and pepper

1 First make the court-bouillon. Place all the ingredients in a large saucepan and gradually bring to the boil. Cover and simmer gently for about 30 minutes. Strain the liquid through a fine sieve into a clean pan. Bring to the boil again and simmer rapidly, uncovered, for 15–20 minutes, until the court-bouillon is reduced to 600 ml/1 pint.

2 Place the trout in a large pan. Add the court-bouillon and gradually bring to the boil. Remove from the heat and leave the fish in the poaching liquid until cold.

3 Meanwhile, make the watercress mayonnaise. Put the egg yolk, mustard, wine vinegar, watercress and seasoning into a food processor or blender and process for 30 seconds, until foaming. Begin adding the olive oil, drop by drop, until the mixture begins to thicken. Continue adding the oil in a slow steady stream until it is all incorporated. Add a little hot water if the mixture seems too thick. Season to taste, cover and chill until required.

4 Cook the potatoes in plenty of lightly salted, boiling water for 12–15 minutes, until soft and tender. Drain well and refresh them under cold running water. Leave the potatoes until cold.

5 When the potatoes are cold, cut them in half if they are very large, and stir into the watercress mayonnaise with the finely chopped spring onions and hard-boiled egg.

6 Carefully lift the fish from the poaching liquid and drain on kitchen paper. Carefully discard the skin from each trout fillet and serve with the potato salad and salad leaves.

herring & potato pie

serves four

1 tbsp Dijon mustard

115 g/4 oz butter, softened

450 g/1 lb herring fillets

750 g/1 lb 10 oz potatoes

1 large onion, sliced

2 cooking apples, sliced thinly

1 tsp chopped fresh sage

600 ml/1 pint hot fish stock

50 g/1¾ oz crustless ciabatta, made
    into breadcrumbs

salt and pepper

fresh parsley sprigs, to garnish

VARIATION

If herrings are unavailable,
substitute mackerel or sardines.

1 Mix the mustard with 25 g/1 oz of the butter until smooth. Spread this mixture over the cut sides of the herring fillets. Season and roll up the fillets. Reserve. Generously grease a 2.2-litres/4-pint pie dish with some of the remaining butter.

2 Thinly slice the potatoes, using a mandolin if possible. Blanch for 3 minutes in plenty of lightly salted, boiling water until just tender. Drain well, refresh under cold water and then pat dry.

3 Heat 25 g/1 oz of the remaining butter in a frying pan and add the onion. Cook gently for 8–10 minutes, until soft but not coloured. Remove from the heat and reserve.

4 Put half the potato slices into the base of the pie dish and season, then add half the apples and half the onion. Put the herring fillets on top of the onion and sprinkle with the sage. Repeat the layers in reverse order, ending with a layer of potato. Season well and add enough hot stock to come halfway up the sides of the dish.

5 Melt the remaining butter and stir in the breadcrumbs until well combined. Sprinkle the breadcrumbs over the pie. Bake in a preheated oven, 190°C/375° F/Gas Mark 5, for about 40–50 minutes, until the breadcrumbs are golden and the herrings are cooked through. Serve immediately garnished with parsley sprigs.

Vegetarian

The potato has become a valued staple of the vegetarian diet, yet anyone who thought this would make for dull eating will be pleasantly surprised by the rich variety of dishes in this chapter. In addition to traditional hearty bakes and hotpots, there are also influences from around the world in dishes such as Tofu & Vegetable Stir-fry from China, and Potato & Cauliflower Curry from India. They all make exciting eating at any time of year.

potato-topped vegetables

serves four

1 carrot, diced

175 g/6 oz cauliflower florets

175 g/6 oz broccoli florets

1 fennel bulb, sliced

75 g/2¾ oz green beans, halved

2 tbsp butter

2½ tbsp plain flour

150 ml/5 fl oz vegetable stock

150 ml/5 fl oz dry white wine

150 ml/5 fl oz milk

175 g/6 oz chestnut
   mushrooms, quartered

2 tbsp chopped fresh sage

TOPPING

900 g/2 lb floury potatoes, diced

2 tbsp butter

4 tbsp natural yogurt

70 g/2½ oz Parmesan cheese,
   freshly grated

1 tsp fennel seeds

salt and pepper

1 Cook the carrot, cauliflower, broccoli, fennel and beans in a large saucepan of boiling water for 10 minutes, until just tender. Drain the vegetables thoroughly and reserve.

2 Melt the butter in a pan. Stir in the flour and cook for 1 minute. Remove from the heat and stir in the stock, wine and milk. Return to the heat and bring to the boil, stirring until thickened. Stir in the reserved vegetables, mushrooms and sage.

3 Meanwhile, make the topping. Cook the potatoes in boiling water for 10–15 minutes. Drain and mash with the butter, yogurt and half the cheese. Stir in the fennel seeds. Season to taste.

4 Spoon the vegetable mixture into a 1-litre/1¾-pints pie dish. Spoon the potato over the top and sprinkle

with the remaining cheese. Cook in a preheated oven, 190°C/375°F/Gas Mark 5, for 30–35 minutes, or until golden. Serve hot.

three cheese soufflé

serves four

2 tbsp butter

2 tsp plain flour

900 g/2 lb floury potatoes

8 eggs, separated

25 g/1 oz Gruyère cheese, grated

25 g/1 oz blue cheese, crumbled

25 g/1 oz mature Cheddar
cheese, grated

salt and pepper

1 Butter a 2.2-litres/4-pints soufflé dish and dust with the flour.

2 Cook the potatoes in a saucepan of boiling water until tender. Mash until very smooth and then transfer to a mixing bowl to cool.

3 Beat the egg yolks into the potato and stir in the Gruyère cheese, blue cheese and Cheddar, mixing well. Season to taste with salt and pepper.

4 Whisk the egg whites until stiff and standing in peaks, gently fold them into the potato mixture with a metal spoon until fully incorporated.

5 Spoon the potato mixture into the prepared soufflé dish.

6 Cook in a preheated oven, 220°C/ 425°F/Gas Mark 7, for 35–40 minutes, until risen and set. Serve immediately.

cheese & potato layer bake

900 g/2 lb unpeeled waxy potatoes,
    cut into wedges

2 tbsp butter

1 red onion, halved and sliced

2 garlic cloves, crushed

2½ tbsp plain flour

600 ml/1 pint milk

400 g/14 oz canned artichoke
    hearts in brine, drained
    and halved

150 g/5½ oz frozen mixed
    vegetables, thawed

125 g/4½ oz Gruyère cheese, grated

125 g/4½ oz mature cheese, grated

50 g/1¾ oz Gorgonzola, crumbled

25 g/1 oz Parmesan cheese,
    freshly grated

225 g/8 oz firm tofu, drained and
    sliced

2 tbsp chopped fresh thyme

salt and pepper

fresh thyme sprigs, to garnish

VARIATION

If you find the flavour of
Gorgonzola too powerful, you
could substitute with the milder-
flavoured docelatte.

---

1 Cook the potato wedges in a saucepan of boiling water for 10 minutes. Drain thoroughly.

2 Meanwhile, melt the butter in a saucepan. Add the sliced onion and garlic and fry over a low heat, stirring frequently, for 2–3 minutes.

3 Stir the flour into the pan and cook for 1 minute. Gradually add the milk, then increase the heat and bring to the boil, stirring constantly.

4 Reduce the heat and add the artichoke hearts, mixed vegetables, half of each of the four cheeses and all the tofu to the pan, mixing well. Stir in the chopped thyme and season with salt and pepper to taste.

5 Arrange a layer of parboiled potato wedges in the base of a shallow ovenproof dish. Spoon the vegetable mixture over the top and cover with the remaining potato wedges. Sprinkle the rest of the four cheeses over the top.

6 Cook in a preheated oven, 200°C/400°F/Gas Mark 6, for 30 minutes, or until the potatoes are cooked and the top is golden brown. Serve the bake garnished with fresh thyme sprigs.

pan potato cake

serves four

675 g/1½ lb waxy potatoes,
   unpeeled and sliced

1 carrot, diced

225 g/8 oz small broccoli florets

5 tbsp butter

2 tbsp vegetable oil

1 red onion, quartered

2 garlic cloves, crushed

175 g/6 oz firm tofu, drained and
   diced

2 tbsp chopped fresh sage

75 g/2¾ oz mature cheese, grated

1 Cook the sliced potatoes in a
large saucepan of boiling water
for 10 minutes. Drain thoroughly.

2 Meanwhile, cook the carrot and
broccoli florets in a separate pan
of boiling water for 5 minutes. Drain
with a slotted spoon.

3 Heat the butter and oil in a
23-cm/9-inch frying pan. Add the
onion and garlic and fry over a low
heat for 2–3 minutes. Add half of the
potato slices to the frying pan,
covering the base of the pan.

4 Cover the potato slices with the
carrot, broccoli and the tofu.
Sprinkle with half of the sage and cover
with the remaining potato slices. Sprinkle
the grated cheese over the top.

5 Cook over a moderate heat for
8–10 minutes. Then place the
pan under a preheated medium grill for
2–3 minutes, or until the cheese melts
and browns.

6 Garnish with the remaining sage
and serve immediately, straight
from the pan.

bubble & squeak

serves four

450 g/1 lb floury potatoes, diced

225 g/8 oz Savoy
   cabbage, shredded

5 tbsp vegetable oil

2 leeks, chopped

1 garlic clove, crushed

225 g/8 oz smoked tofu, drained
   and diced

salt and pepper

shredded cooked leek, to garnish

COOK'S TIP

This is a perfect main meal,
because the smoked tofu cubes
added to the basic bubble and
squeak mixture make it very
substantial and nourishing.

1 Cook the diced potatoes in a
saucepan of lightly salted, boiling
water for 10 minutes, until tender.
Drain and mash the potatoes.

2 Meanwhile, in a separate
saucepan, blanch the cabbage
in boiling water for 5 minutes. Drain
well and add to the potato.

3 Heat the oil in a large, heavy-
based frying pan. Add the leeks
and garlic and fry over a low heat for
2–3 minutes. Stir into the potato and
cabbage mixture.

4 Add the smoked tofu and season
well with salt and pepper. Cook
over a moderate heat for 10 minutes.

5 Carefully turn the whole mixture
over and continue to cook over a
moderate heat for 5–7 minutes more,
until it is crispy underneath.

6 Serve immediately, garnished
with shredded leek.

potato-topped lentil bake

TOPPING

675 g/1½ lb floury potatoes, diced

2 tbsp butter

1 tbsp milk

50 g/1¾ oz pecan nuts, chopped

2 tbsp chopped fresh thyme

fresh thyme sprigs, to garnish

FILLING

225 g/8 oz red lentils

5 tbsp butter

1 leek, sliced

2 garlic cloves, crushed

1 celery stick, chopped

125 g/4½ oz broccoli florets

175 g/6 oz smoked tofu, diced

2 tsp tomato purée

salt and pepper

COOK'S TIP

Tofu is quite delicate, so always use a very sharp knife when dicing or slicing it. A blunt knife would squash it.

1 To make the topping, cook the potatoes in a saucepan of boiling water for 10–15 minutes, or until cooked through. Drain well, add the butter and milk and mash thoroughly. Stir in the pecan nuts and chopped thyme and reserve.

2 Cook the lentils in boiling water for 20–30 minutes, or until tender. Drain and reserve.

3 Melt the butter in a frying pan. Add the leek, garlic, celery and broccoli. Fry over a medium heat, stirring frequently, for 5 minutes, until softened. Add the tofu cubes. Stir in

VARIATION

You can use almost any combination of your favourite vegetables in this dish.

the lentils, together with the tomato purée. Season with salt and pepper to taste, then turn the mixture into the base of a shallow ovenproof dish.

4 Spoon the mashed potato on top of the lentil mixture, spreading to cover it completely.

5 Cook in a preheated oven, 200°C/ 400°F/Gas Mark 6, for about 30–35 minutes, or until the topping is golden. Garnish with sprigs of fresh thyme and serve hot.

cauliflower bake

serves four

500 g/1 lb 2 oz cauliflower, broken
into florets

600 g/1 lb 5 oz potatoes, diced

100 g/3½ oz cherry tomatoes

SAUCE

2 tbsp butter or margarine

1 leek, sliced

1 garlic clove, crushed

3 tbsp plain flour

300 ml/10 fl oz milk

75 g/2¾ oz mixed cheese, such
as Cheddar, Parmesan and
Gruyère, grated

½ tsp paprika

2 tbsp chopped fresh flat-
leaved parsley

salt and pepper

chopped fresh parsley, to garnish

1. Cook the cauliflower in boiling water for 10 minutes. Drain well and reserve. Meanwhile, cook the potatoes in a pan of boiling water for 10 minutes, drain and reserve.

2. To make the sauce, melt the butter or margarine in a saucepan and sauté the leek and garlic for 1 minute. Stir in the flour and cook, stirring constantly, for 1 minute. Remove the pan from the heat and gradually stir in the milk, 50 g/ 1¾ oz of the cheese, the paprika and parsley. Return the pan to the heat and bring to the boil, stirring constantly. Season with salt and pepper to taste.

3. Spoon the cauliflower into a deep ovenproof dish. Add the cherry tomatoes and top with the potatoes. Pour the sauce over the potatoes and sprinkle on the remaining cheese.

4. Cook in a preheated oven, 180°C/ 350°F/Gas Mark 4, for 20 minutes, or until the vegetables are cooked through and the cheese is golden brown and bubbling. Garnish and serve immediately.

nutty harvest loaf

serves four

2 tbsp butter, plus extra for greasing

450 g/1 lb floury potatoes, diced

1 onion, chopped

2 garlic cloves, crushed

125 g/4½ oz unsalted peanuts

75 g/2¾ oz fresh white
    breadcrumbs

1 egg, beaten

2 tbsp chopped fresh coriander

150 ml/5 fl oz vegetable stock

75 g/2¾ oz sliced mushrooms

50 g/1¾ oz sun-dried tomatoes in
    oil, drained and sliced

salt and pepper

SAUCE

150 ml/5 fl oz crème fraîche

2 tsp tomato purée

2 tsp clear honey

2 tbsp chopped fresh coriander

1 Grease a 450 g/1 lb loaf tin.
Cook the potatoes in a saucepan
of lightly salted boiling water for 10
minutes, until cooked through. Drain
well, mash and reserve.

2 Melt half of the butter in a frying
pan. Add the onion and garlic
and fry gently for 2–3 minutes, until
soft. Finely chop the nuts or process
them in a food processor for about
30 seconds with the breadcrumbs.

3 Mix the chopped nuts and
breadcrumbs into the potatoes
with the egg, coriander and vegetable
stock. Stir in the onion and garlic,
season to taste and mix well.

4 Melt the remaining butter in
the frying pan, add the sliced
mushrooms and cook for 2–3 minutes.

5 Press half of the potato mixture
into the base of the loaf tin.
Spoon the mushrooms on top and
sprinkle with the sun-dried tomatoes.
Spoon the remaining potato mixture
on top and smooth the surface. Cover
with foil and bake in a preheated oven,
190°C/375°F/Gas Mark 5, for 1 hour,
or until firm to the touch.

6 Meanwhile, mix the sauce
ingredients together. Cut the
nutty harvest loaf into slices and
serve with the sauce.

potato & aubergine gratin

serves four

500 g/1 lb 2 oz waxy
   potatoes, sliced

1 tbsp vegetable oil

1 onion, chopped

2 garlic cloves, crushed

500 g/1 lb 2 oz firm tofu, drained
   and diced

2 tbsp tomato purée

2 tbsp plain flour

300 ml/10 fl oz vegetable stock

2 large tomatoes, sliced

1 aubergine, sliced

2 tbsp chopped fresh thyme

450 ml/16 fl oz natural yogurt

2 eggs, beaten

salt and pepper

VARIATION

You can use marinated or smoked tofu for extra flavour, if you wish.

---

1 Cook the sliced potatoes in a saucepan of boiling water for 10 minutes, until tender but not breaking up. Drain and reserve.

2 Heat the oil in a frying pan. Add the onion and garlic and fry, stirring occasionally, for 2–3 minutes.

3 Add the tofu, tomato purée and flour and cook for 1 minute. Gradually stir in the stock and bring to the boil, stirring. Reduce the heat and simmer for 10 minutes.

4 Arrange a layer of the potato slices in the base of a deep ovenproof dish. Spoon the tofu mixture evenly on top. Layer the sliced tomatoes, then the aubergine and finally, the remaining potato slices on top of the tofu mixture, making sure that it is completely covered. Sprinkle with thyme.

5 Mix the yogurt and beaten eggs together in a bowl and season to taste with salt and pepper. Spoon the yogurt topping over the sliced potatoes to cover them completely.

6 Bake in a preheated oven, 190°C/375°F/Gas Mark 5, for about 35–45 minutes, or until the topping is browned. Serve the gratin immediately with a crisp salad.

stuffed rice pancakes

200 g/7 oz rice and 50 g/1¾ oz urid
   dhal, or 200 g/7 oz ground rice
   and 50 g/1¾ oz urid dhal
   flour (ata)

425–600 ml/15 fl oz–1 pint water

1 tsp salt

4 tbsp vegetable oil

coriander sprigs to garnish

FILLING

900 g/2 lb potatoes, diced

3 fresh green chillies, deseeded
   and chopped

½ tsp ground turmeric

1 tsp salt

150 ml/5 fl oz vegetable oil

1 tsp mixed mustard and
   onion seeds

3 dried red chillies

4 curry leaves

2 tbsp lemon juice

COOK'S TIP

Specialist Indian flours and
mustard and onion seeds are
available from some large
supermarkets and from Indian
food stores.

---

1 To make the dosas – pancakes –
soak the rice and urid dhal for
3 hours. Grind the rice and urid dhal
to a smooth consistency, adding water
if necessary. Leave for a further
3 hours to ferment. Alternatively, if you
are using ground rice and urid dhal
flour (ata), mix together in a bowl. Add
the water and salt and stir until a
batter is formed.

2 Heat about 1 tablespoon of oil
in a large, non-stick, frying-pan.
Using a ladle, spoon the batter into the
frying-pan. Tilt the frying-pan to spread
the mixture over the base. Cover and
cook over a medium heat for about
2 minutes. Remove the lid and turn the
dosa over very carefully. Pour a little oil
around the edge, cover and cook for a
further 2 minutes. Repeat with the
remaining batter.

3 To make the filling, cook the
potatoes in a pan of boiling
water. Add the green chillies, turmeric
and salt and cook until the potatoes
are just soft. Drain and mash lightly
with a fork.

4 Heat the vegetable oil in a
saucepan and fry the mustard
and onion seeds, dried red chillies and
curry leaves, stirring constantly, for
about 1 minute. Pour the spice mixture
over the mashed potatoes, then
sprinkle over the lemon juice and mix
well. Spoon the potato filling on one
half of each of the dosas and fold the
other half over it. Transfer to a warmed
serving dish, garnish and serve hot.

potato & vegetable curry

serves four

4 tbsp vegetable oil

675 g/1½ lb waxy potatoes, cut into
    large chunks

2 onions, quartered

3 garlic cloves, crushed

1 tsp garam masala

½ tsp ground turmeric

½ tsp ground cumin

½ tsp ground coriander

2 tsp grated fresh root ginger

1 fresh red chilli, deseeded
    and chopped

225 g/8 oz cauliflower florets

4 tomatoes, skinned and quartered

75 g/2¾ oz frozen peas

2 tbsp chopped fresh coriander

300 ml10 fl oz vegetable stock

shredded fresh coriander,
    to garnish

boiled rice or Indian bread, to serve

COOK'S TIP

Use a large heavy-based
saucepan or frying pan for this
recipe to ensure that the
potatoes are cooked thoroughly.

---

1 Heat the vegetable oil in a large heavy-based saucepan or frying pan. Add the potato chunks, onions and garlic and fry over a low heat, stirring frequently, for 2–3 minutes.

2 Add the garam masala, turmeric, ground cumin, ground coriander, ginger and chilli to the pan, mixing the spices into the vegetables. Fry over a low heat, stirring constantly, for 1 minute.

3 Add the cauliflower florets, tomato quarters, peas and chopped coriander to the curry mixture and stir well. Pour in the vegetable stock and stir again.

4 Cook the potato curry over a low heat for 30–40 minutes, or until the potatoes are tender and completely cooked through.

5 Garnish the potato curry with fresh coriander and serve with plain boiled rice or warm Indian bread.

chickpea curry

serves four

6 tbsp vegetable oil

2 onions, sliced

1 tsp finely chopped fresh
   root ginger

1 tsp ground cumin

1 tsp ground coriander

1 tsp fresh garlic, crushed

1 tsp chilli powder

2 fresh green chillies

1 tbsp fresh coriander leaves

150 ml/5 fl oz water

300 g/10½ oz potatoes

400 g/14 oz canned chickpeas,
   drained and rinsed

1 tbsp lemon or lime juice

chapatis, to serve (optional)

1 Heat the oil in a large saucepan over a medium heat.

2 Add the onions to the pan and fry, stirring occasionally, until they are golden brown.

3 Reduce the heat, add the ginger, ground cumin, ground coriander, garlic, chilli powder, fresh green chillies and fresh coriander leaves to the pan and stir-fry for 2 minutes.

4 Add the water to the mixture in the pan and stir to mix.

5 Using a sharp knife, cut the potatoes into small cubes.

6 Add the potatoes and chickpeas to the mixture in the pan, cover and simmer, stirring occasionally, for 5–7 minutes.

7 Sprinkle the lemon or lime juice over the curry.

8 Transfer the chickpea curry to serving dishes. Serve the curry hot with chapatis, if you wish.

potato curry

3 medium potatoes

150 ml/5 fl oz vegetable oil

1 tsp onion seeds

½ tsp fennel seeds

4 curry leaves

1 tsp ground cumin

1 tsp ground coriander

1 tsp chilli powder

pinch of ground turmeric

1 tsp salt

1½ tsp dried mango powder

1 Peel and rinse the potatoes. Using a sharp knife, cut each potato into 6 slices.

2 Cook the potato slices in a saucepan of boiling water until just cooked, but not mushy (test by piercing with the point of a sharp knife or a skewer). Drain well, cover lightly and leave until required.

3 Heat the vegetable oil in a separate, heavy-based saucepan over a moderate heat. Reduce the heat and add the onion seeds, fennel seeds and curry leaves and stir thoroughly.

4 Remove the pan from the heat and add the ground cumin, coriander, chilli powder, turmeric, salt and dried mango powder, stirring well to combine.

5 Return the pan to a low heat and fry the mixture, stirring constantly, for about 1 minute.

6 Pour this mixture over the cooked potatoes, mix together and stir-fry over a low heat for about 5 minutes.

7 Transfer the potato curry to serving dishes and serve immediately.

vegetable pulao

serves six

450 g/1 lb potatoes, cut into

    12 pieces

1 aubergine, cut into 6 pieces

2 carrots, sliced

50 g/1¾ oz green beans, chopped

4 tbsp vegetable ghee

2 onions, sliced

175 ml/6 fl oz natural yogurt

2 tsp finely chopped fresh

    root ginger

2 tsp crushed garlic

2 tsp garam masala

2 tsp black cumin seeds

½ tsp ground turmeric

3 black cardamom pods

3 cinnamon sticks

2 tsp salt

1 tsp chilli powder

½ tsp saffron threads

300 ml/10 fl oz milk

600 g/1 lb 5 oz basmati rice

5 tbsp lemon juice

TO GARNISH

4 fresh green chillies, deseeded

    and chopped

fresh coriander leaves,

    chopped finely

1 Have the prepared vegetables to hand. Heat the ghee in a pan. Add the potatoes, aubergine, carrots and beans and fry, turning frequently, until softened. Remove from the pan and drain well.

2 Add the onions to the pan, and fry, stirring frequently, until soft. Add the yogurt, ginger, garlic, garam masala, 1 teaspoon black cumin seeds, the turmeric, 1 cardamom pod, 1 cinnamon stick, 1 teaspoon salt and the chilli powder and stir-fry for 3–5 minutes. Return the vegetables to the pan and fry for 4–5 minutes.

3 Put the saffron and milk in a saucepan and bring to the boil, stirring. Remove from the heat and leave to cool.

4 In a pan of boiling water, half-cook the rice with 1 teaspoon salt, 2 cinnamon sticks, 2 black cardamom pods and 1 teaspoon black cumin seeds. Drain the rice, leaving half in the pan, while transferring the other half to a bowl. Pour the vegetable mixture on top of the rice in the pan. Pour half of the lemon juice and half of the saffron milk over the vegetables and rice, then cover with the remaining rice and pour the remaining lemon juice and saffron milk over the top.

5 Garnish with chopped green chillies and fresh coriander, return to the heat and cover. Cook over a low heat for about 20 minutes. Serve the pulao while hot.

tofu & vegetable stir-fry

serves four

175 g/6 oz potatoes, diced

1 tbsp vegetable oil

1 red onion, sliced

225 g/8 oz firm tofu, drained and
    diced

2 courgettes, diced

8 canned artichoke hearts, halved

150 ml/5 fl oz passata

1 tbsp sweet chilli sauce

1 tbsp soy sauce

1 tsp caster sugar

2 tbsp chopped fresh basil

salt and pepper

1 Cook the potatoes in boiling water for 10 minutes. Drain thoroughly and leave until required.

2 Heat the vegetable oil in a wok or large frying pan and sauté the red onion for 2 minutes, until the onion has softened, stirring.

3 Stir in the tofu and courgettes and cook for 3–4 minutes, until they begin to brown slightly.

4 Add the cooked potatoes to the wok or frying pan, stirring to mix.

5 Stir in the artichoke hearts, passata, sweet chilli sauce, soy sauce, sugar and basil.

6 Season to taste with salt and pepper and cook for a further 5 minutes, stirring well.

7 Transfer the tofu and vegetable stir-fry to warmed serving dishes and serve immediately.

mixed vegetables

300 ml/10 fl oz vegetable oil

1 tsp mustard seeds

1 tsp onion seeds

½ tsp white cumin seeds

3–4 curry leaves, chopped

450 g/1 lb onions, chopped finely

3 tomatoes, chopped

½ red and ½ green pepper,
  deseeded and sliced

1 tsp finely chopped fresh
  root ginger

1 tsp crushed garlic

1 tsp chilli powder

¼ tsp ground turmeric

1 tsp salt

425 ml/15 fl oz water

450 g/1 lb potatoes, cut into pieces

½ cauliflower, cut into small florets

4 carrots, peeled and sliced

3 fresh green chillies, deseeded and
  chopped finely

1 tbsp fresh coriander leaves

1 tbsp lemon juice

1 Heat the oil in a large saucepan. Add the mustard, onion and white cumin seeds along with the curry leaves and fry until they turn a shade darker.

2 Add the onions to the pan and fry over a medium heat until golden brown.

3 Add the tomatoes and red and green peppers and stir-fry for about 5 minutes.

4 Add the ginger, garlic, chilli powder, turmeric and salt and mix well.

5 Add 300 ml/10 fl oz of the water, cover and simmer for about 10–12 minutes, stirring occasionally.

6 Add the potatoes, cauliflower, carrots, green chillies and coriander leaves and stir-fry for about 5 minutes.

7 Add the remaining water and the lemon juice, stirring to combine. Cover and simmer for about 15 minutes, stirring occasionally.

8 Transfer the mixed vegetables to warmed serving plates and serve immediately.

potato & cauliflower curry

150 ml/5 fl oz vegetable oil

½ tsp white cumin seeds

4 dried red chillies

2 onions, sliced

1 tsp finely chopped fresh
   root ginger

1 tsp crushed garlic

1 tsp chilli powder

1 tsp salt

pinch of ground turmeric

675 g/1 lb 8 oz potatoes, chopped

½ cauliflower, cut into small florets

2 fresh green chillies (optional)

1 tbsp fresh coriander leaves

150 ml/5 fl oz water

COOK'S TIP

Ground ginger is no substitute
for the fresh root. It is less
aromatic and flavoursome and
cannot be used in fried or
sautéed dishes, because it
burns easily at the high
temperatures required.

1 Heat the oil in a large, heavy-
based saucepan. Add the white
cumin seeds and dried red chillies to
the pan, stirring to mix.

2 Add the onions to the pan and
fry over a medium heat, stirring
occasionally, for about 5–8 minutes,
until golden brown.

3 Mix the ginger, garlic, chilli
powder, salt and turmeric
together. Add the spice mixture to the
onions and stir-fry for about 2 minutes.

4 Add the potatoes and cauliflower
to the pan and stir to coat
thoroughly with the spice mixture.
Reduce the heat and add the green
chillies (if using), coriander leaves and
water to the pan. Cover and simmer
for about 10–15 minutes, until the
vegetables are cooked right through
and are tender.

5 Transfer the potato and
cauliflower curry to warmed
serving plates and serve immediately.

yellow curry

serves four

2 garlic cloves, finely chopped

3-cm/1¼-inch piece galangal, chopped finely

1 lemon grass stalk, chopped finely

1 tsp coriander seeds

3 tbsp vegetable oil

2 tsp Thai red curry paste

½ tsp ground turmeric

200 ml/7 fl oz coconut milk

250 g/9 oz potatoes, diced

100 ml/3½ fl oz vegetable stock

200 g/7 oz young spinach leaves

1 small onion, sliced thinly into rings

1 Place the garlic, galangal, lemon grass and coriander seeds in a mortar and pound with a pestle to a smooth paste.

2 Heat 2 tablespoons of the oil in a frying pan or wok. Stir in the garlic paste and stir-fry for 30 seconds. Stir in the curry paste and turmeric, then add the coconut milk and bring the mixture to the boil.

3 Add the potatoes and stock. Return to the boil, then lower the heat and simmer, uncovered, for 10–12 minutes, until the potatoes are almost tender.

4 Stir in the spinach and simmer until the leaves are wilted.

5 Fry the onion in the remaining oil until crisp and golden brown. Place on top of the curry just before serving.

COOK'S TIP

Choose a firm, waxy potato for this dish, one that will keep its shape during cooking, in preference to a floury variety that will break up easily once cooked.

potato & lemon casserole

serves four

100 ml/3½ fl oz olive oil

2 red onions, cut into 8 wedges

3 garlic cloves, crushed

2 tsp ground cumin

2 tsp ground coriander

pinch of cayenne pepper

1 carrot, sliced thickly

2 small turnips, quartered

1 courgette, sliced

500 g/1 lb 2 oz potatoes,
  sliced thickly

juice and grated rind of
  2 large lemons

300 ml/10 fl oz vegetable stock

2 tbsp chopped fresh coriander

salt and pepper

COOK'S TIP

Check the vegetables while they
are cooking because they may
begin to stick to the pan.
Add a little more boiling water
or stock if necessary.

2 Add the garlic and cook for
30 seconds. Stir in the spices and
cook, stirring constantly, for 1 minute.

3 Add the carrot, turnips, courgette
and potatoes and stir to coat in
the oil.

4 Add the lemon juice and grated
rind and the vegetable stock.
Season to taste with salt and pepper.
Cover and cook over a medium heat,
stirring occasionally, for about
20–30 minutes, until tender.

5 Remove the lid, sprinkle in the
chopped coriander and stir well.
Serve immediately.

1 Heat the olive oil in a flameproof
casserole. Add the onions and
sauté over a medium heat, stirring
frequently, for 3 minutes.

Baking

The potato adds an interesting flavour and texture to loaves and cakes. This section includes a range of unusual recipes, and also shows the qualities of the sweet potato in combination with fruit and spices, such as the Fruity Potato Cake, which is ideal for any special occasion. There is also a tempting plaited loaf and some smaller treats, such as Potato Muffins and the delicately spiced Potato & Nutmeg Scones.

cheese & potato plait

serves eight

butter, for greasing

175 g/6 oz floury potatoes, diced

2 x 7 g sachets easy-blend
   dried yeast

675 g/1 lb 8 oz strong white bread
   flour, plus extra for dusting

1 tbsp salt

450 ml/16 fl oz vegetable stock

2 garlic cloves, crushed

2 tbsp chopped fresh rosemary

125 g/4½ oz grated Gruyère cheese

1 tbsp vegetable oil

COOK'S TIP

When cooking with yeast, the temperature of the other ingredients is critical. If the mixture is too hot, the yeast will be killed; if it is too cold, it will not be activated. Let the mashed potatoes cool to hand-hot before mixing in the yeast in step 2. Remove the vegetable stock from the refrigerator and leave to stand for 30 minutes to come to room temperature before using.

1 Lightly grease and flour a baking tray. Cook the potatoes in a pan of boiling water for 10 minutes, or until soft. Drain and mash.

2 Transfer the mashed potatoes to a large mixing bowl, stir in the yeast, flour, salt and stock and mix to form a smooth dough. Add the garlic, rosemary and 75 g/2¾ oz of the cheese and knead the dough on a lightly floured surface for 5 minutes. Make a hollow in the dough, pour in the oil and knead the dough again.

3 Cover the dough and leave it to rise in a warm place for 1½ hours, or until doubled in size.

4 Knead the dough again and divide it into 3 equal portions. Roll each portion into a sausage shape about 35 cm/14 inches long.

5 Press one end of each of the sausage shapes firmly together, then carefully plait the dough, without breaking it, and fold the remaining ends under, sealing them firmly.

6 Place the plait on the baking tray, cover and leave to rise for 30 minutes.

7 Sprinkle the remaining cheese over the top of the plait and cook in a preheated oven, 190°C/375°F/Gas Mark 5, for 40 minutes, or until the base of the loaf sounds hollow when tapped. Serve while it is warm.

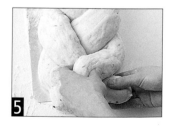

potato muffins

serves twelve

butter, for greasing

85 g/3 oz self-raising flour, plus
extra for dusting

175 g/6 oz floury potatoes, diced

2 tbsp soft light brown sugar

1 tsp baking powder

125 g/4½ oz raisins

4 eggs, separated

COOK'S TIP

Instead of spreading the muffins
with plain butter, serve them
with cinnamon butter made
by blending 5 tablespoons
butter with a large pinch of
ground cinnamon.

1 Lightly grease and flour 12 muffin
tins. Cook the diced potatoes
in a saucepan of boiling water for
10 minutes, or until cooked. Drain well
and mash until smooth.

2 Transfer the mashed potatoes to
a mixing bowl and add the flour,
sugar, baking powder, raisins and egg
yolks. Stir well to mix thoroughly.

3 In a clean bowl, whisk the egg
whites until stiff and standing in
soft peaks. Using a metal spoon, gently
fold them into the potato mixture until
fully incorporated.

 Divide the mixture among the
prepared tins.

5 Cook the muffins in a preheated
oven, 200°C/400°F/Gas Mark 6,
for 10 minutes. Reduce the oven
temperature to 160°C/325°F/Gas
Mark 3 and cook the muffins for a
further 7–10 minutes, or until risen.

6 Remove the muffins from the tins
and serve warm.

potato & nutmeg scones

serves eight

butter, for greasing

225 g/8 oz floury potatoes, diced

125 g/4½ oz plain flour

1½ tsp baking powder

½ tsp grated nutmeg

50 g/1¾ oz sultanas

1 egg, beaten

3 tbsp double cream

2 tsp soft light brown sugar

COOK'S TIP

For extra convenience, make a batch of scones in advance and freeze them. Thaw thoroughly and warm in a moderate oven when ready to serve.

1 Line and grease a baking tray. Cook the diced potatoes in a saucepan of boiling water for 10 minutes, or until soft. Drain well and mash the potatoes.

2 Transfer the mashed potatoes to a large mixing bowl and stir in the flour, baking powder and nutmeg.

3 Stir in the sultanas, egg and cream and beat the mixture with a wooden spoon until smooth.

4 Shape the mixture into 8 rounds about 2 cm/¾ inch thick and place on the baking tray.

5 Cook in a preheated oven, 200°C/400°F/Gas Mark 6, for about 15 minutes, or until the scones have risen and are cooked and golden. Sprinkle the scones with sugar and serve warm spread with butter.

fruity potato cake

1 tbsp butter, melted, plus extra
   for greasing
675 g/1lb 8 oz sweet potatoes
125 g/4½ oz demerara sugar
3 eggs
3 tbsp skimmed milk
1 tbsp lemon juice
grated rind of 1 lemon
1 tsp caraway seeds
125 g/4½ oz dried fruit, such as
   apple, pear or mango, chopped
2 tsp baking powder
thick cream, to serve (optional)

1 Lightly grease an 18-cm/7-inch square cake tin.

2 Dice and cook the sweet potatoes in a large saucepan of boiling water for 10 minutes, or until soft. Drain and mash until smooth.

3 Transfer the mashed potatoes to a mixing bowl while still hot and add the butter and sugar, mixing together well to dissolve the sugar.

4 Beat in the eggs, milk, lemon juice and rind, caraway seeds and chopped dried fruit. Add the baking powder and mix well.

5 Pour the mixture into the prepared cake tin.

6 Cook in a preheated oven, 160°C/ 325°F/Gas Mark 3, for 1–1¼ hours, or until cooked through.

7 Remove the cake from the tin and cool on a wire rack. Slice and serve with the cream if using.

sweet potato bread

5 tbsp butter, plus extra for greasing

225 g/8 oz sweet potatoes, diced

150 ml/5 fl oz hand-hot water

2 tbsp clear honey

2 tbsp vegetable oil

3 tbsp orange juice

75 g/2¾ oz semolina

225 g/8 oz strong white
bread flour

1 x 7 g sachet dried yeast

1 tsp ground cinnamon

grated rind of 1 orange

1 Lightly grease a 675 g/1 lb 8 oz loaf tin. Cook the sweet potatoes in a saucepan of boiling water for about 10 minutes, or until soft. Drain well and mash until smooth.

2 Meanwhile, mix the water, honey, oil and orange juice together in a large mixing bowl.

3 Add the mashed sweet potatoes, semolina, three-quarters of the flour, the yeast, ground cinnamon and grated orange rind and mix thoroughly to form a dough. Leave to stand for about 10 minutes.

4 Cut the butter into small pieces and knead it into the dough with the remaining flour. Knead for about 5 minutes, until the dough is smooth.

5 Place the dough in the prepared loaf tin. Cover and leave in a warm place to rise for 1 hour, or until the dough has doubled in size.

6 Cook the loaf in a preheated oven, 190°C/375°F/Gas Mark 5, for 45–60 minutes, or until the base sounds hollow when tapped. Serve the bread warm, cut into slices.